STRONG INSIDE

STRONG INSIDE

The True Story of How Perry Wallace
Broke College Basketball's Color Line

ANDREW MARANISS

PHILOMEL BOOKS

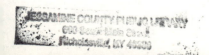

PHILOMEL BOOKS
an imprint of Penguin Random House LLC
375 Hudson Street
New York, NY 10014

Copyright © 2017 by Andrew Maraniss. Adaped for young people from *Strong Inside: Perry Wallace and the Collision of Race and Sports in the South* published by Vanderbilt University Press in 2014. Cover art inspired by a photo copyright © *The Tennessean.*

Printed in the United States of America.
ISBN 9780399548345
3 5 7 9 10 8 6 4 2

Edited by Brian Geffen.
Design by Kimi Weart.
Text set in Columbus.

For Alison, Eliza, and Charlie—my favorite team

CONTENTS

Dear Readers: To accurately and vividly convey the racism that Perry Wallace and others encountered during certain scenes described in this book, the derogatory language they heard at the time is included here without edits. It would be a disservice to the reader and the heroes of this story to whitewash history by sanitizing these epithets.

Chapter 1

A Dangerous Place

IF YOU TAKE A LOOK at the Vanderbilt University basketball schedule for the 1966–67 season and search for the game dated February 27, you'll see it was the day the Vanderbilt Commodores traveled to Starkville, Mississippi, to play the Mississippi State Bulldogs. But that day meant something much different to one member of the Vanderbilt basketball team.

For Perry Wallace, February 27, 1967, will always be remembered as the day he visited hell on earth.

From the very moment Vanderbilt's flight from Nashville landed in Mississippi, a dangerous place for African Americans ever since the days of slavery, it was obvious the plane had delivered Wallace and his only other black teammate, Godfrey Dillard, straight into the heart of intolerance.

When the small propeller plane landed on a gravel runway surrounded by tall trees, Dillard thought, *This place is backwoods*. From the airport, a bus delivered the Commodores to their hotel, where a group of white students milled around, yelling at Wallace and Dillard and banging on the bus. As the Vanderbilt players walked into the Holiday Inn, all the white folks in the lobby turned around and stared at the two black players. They could not have felt more unwelcome.

Sleep did not come easily for Wallace and Dillard that night. As members of Vanderbilt's freshman basketball team (in those days, freshmen couldn't play on the varsity), they were about to become the first African American basketball players ever to play a Southeastern Conference game in the state of Mississippi.

Prior to the trip, Wallace told a Nashville sportswriter that he hadn't thought much about what might lay ahead in Starkville. "Schoolwork and basketball practice keep a man's mind on other things," he said. "However, I certainly do wonder just what sort of reception we'll get."

In truth, Wallace had thought quite a bit about the trip, bracing himself for the hatred he suspected he and Dillard would encounter. "You knew you were going to get hit in some way," he recalled years later. "It was just a question of how bad was it going to be."

On game day, Wallace contemplated his surroundings. He was troubled by what he knew of Mississippi: less than three years had passed since three young civil rights workers had been murdered only about sixty miles from Starkville, and less than a year had passed since James Meredith, the first black student to attend the University of Mississippi, was shot in broad daylight, even while surrounded by FBI agents. But it wasn't what he knew that concerned Wallace the most; it was the *unknown*.

"That's the problem for pioneers," he recalled. "You don't know what could possibly happen to you. When you don't know what's going to happen, the sky is the limit."

It is possible that the cramped visitors' locker room in the bowels of the Mississippi State gym was *always* a stinking mess, but when Godfrey Dillard and Perry Wallace walked in, they took stock of the filthy surroundings and believed that what they saw and smelled was an attack directed squarely at them, a pair of unwanted guests: there were toilets overflowing, towels scattered everywhere across a dirty floor.

Game time approached, and the Commodores made their way from the locker room to the portal that led to the court, most of the players mentally preparing for a basketball game, Dillard and Wallace bracing themselves for the unknown, feeling like they were at the very apex of a roller coaster, their stomachs briefly suspended as if at zero gravity.

And then out of the tunnel and onto the court and, *boom*, the sensation of the rapid drop, the too-bright arena lights searing their eyes, the ringing of cowbells (a Mississippi State tradition), the piercing screams from the fans jammed close to the court, flashes of light and sound and eruptions of hate from every direction. Two young black kids exposed and surrounded in the heart of Mississippi, there for the taking.

Go home, niggers! We're going to kill you, coons! We're gonna lynch you! Forty years later, the scene stood out in teammate Bob Bundy's mind; in his memory, as the Commodore freshmen warmed up under one basket, the whole bleachers were full of Mississippi State football players screaming at Perry and Godfrey. When Vanderbilt switched baskets, the football players followed them across the gym, continuing their threats.

Wallace's blood ran cold; he had trouble gripping the basketball, his fingers gone stiff and numb. His mind raced to scenes from his childhood: the carload of punks who pointed a gun at him as he waited for the bus, the bullies who harassed him as he walked to school. He had seen racism bring out the worst in people.

But this was a whole new level of hate.

What had he gotten himself into?

Chapter 2

Short 26th

BEFORE THAT UGLY DAY IN Starkville, before Perry Eugene Wallace Jr. even came into this world, there was Short 26th, just a stub of a road in Nashville, Tennessee. Perry's story begins in a little house on a dead-end street on the other side of the tracks.

His parents, Perry Wallace Sr. and Hattie Haynes Wallace, had come to Nashville from rural Rutherford County, Tennessee, not long after their marriage in 1928.

The Wallaces lived in North Nashville, the city's center of black life, and one road—Jefferson Street—was the place where everything happened. In a segregated society where whites treated blacks as second-class citizens, this was where Black Power, a movement that emphasized self-empowerment for African Americans, flourished long before the slogan was invented. Living in the "black cocoon," as Perry Wallace described it, meant buying from black-owned businesses, entering the front doors of black movie theaters, eating in black restaurants. Inside the cocoon, poor as it was, there were no whites-only lunch counters or back-alley entrances. Rather, there were black institutions like Isom's Beauty Shop, Frank White's Cleaners, and the Ritz Theater. The leading black entertainers of the mid-twentieth century, from Duke Ellington, Count Basie, and Nat King Cole to Little Richard and Ella Fitzgerald, included Nashville on their tours.

Perry Sr. and Hattie made a life in this cocoon. It was humble—this was *Short* 26th after all. Their house was small—living room, bedroom, kitchen, bedroom, porch—but soon enough it filled up with kids. First there was Annie, who became known simply as Sister, and then along came James, known as Brother, and Bessie, Jessie, and Ruby Jean.

Perry Sr. and Hattie lived a wholesome life, and they were determined, despite the temptations of the city, that their children would do the same. Of all the traditions and values in the Wallace home, the two most important were religion and education. The children went to Sunday school, read the Bible, and attended services with their mother. The Wallaces believed that a strong education was a necessary ingredient if their children were to succeed in a society that not only was becoming more fast-paced but also was engineered to restrict opportunities for black people. The Wallace kids were smart, so smart that they encountered more than a few strange looks from some neighbors. Were those really French-, Spanish-, and German-language records you could hear Annie practicing with when you walked past the little house on Short 26th? What was *that* all about? That family was *different.*

On February 19, 1948, this straitlaced family of seven got quite a surprise: Perry Eugene Wallace Jr. was born at Meharry Hospital.

Can a birth really be that much of a surprise?

For some, it was quite unexpected, given that the eldest Wallace child, Annie, was a sophomore in college and the youngest, Ruby Jean, had been born ten years earlier.

As his older brother and sisters eventually all moved out of the house, Perry became extremely close to his parents; the love and values Hattie passed along to her son began to shape his behavior. In a world of chaos, much of it soon to be directed at him, he would remain above the fray. Some observers would later remark on Perry's unflappable character when they saw him remain cool under pressure in hostile places like Oxford, Mississippi, and Auburn, Alabama.

They should have seen him in kindergarten.

Perry Wallace's education began in 1954, the same year as the famous Supreme Court decision *Brown v. Board of Education* made segregation illegal in schools. Before that time, "separate but equal" had been the way of life in many parts of the country, which meant that white people and black people had to sit in separate parts of the bus, use separate bathrooms, drink from separate water fountains, and attend different schools. Of course, there was nothing equal about it at all—it was racial discrimination, plain and simple, and African Americans were treated as inferior. Now that separate but equal was against the law, it was supposed to be the beginning of a new, more equal and fair era in America.

But change takes time to catch hold, so every day Perry the kindergartner walked from Short 26th over to the all-black Jewel's Academy, a private school run by the Church of God in Christ. Whether it was the imposing figure of Chief Jewel, the female bishop who ran the school, or the lessons on respect he had learned from his parents, Perry was the best-behaved kid in kindergarten. This didn't necessarily sit well with his sister Jessie, who occasionally picked up her little brother from school.

Jessie arrived at Perry's classroom one day, and the teacher was nowhere in sight. The kids were going berserk, running around screaming, bouncing off walls and windows. All but one kid, that is. As his classmates went bonkers, there at his tiny desk sat Perry Wallace, not saying a word, waiting patiently for his sister.

"I was just enraged, not at the children, but at the teacher," Jessie recalled. "But my strongest feeling of all was, 'Is my brother going to be a wimp? Is he going to stand up for himself with these rougher guys? Is he going to be able to defend himself?'

"I think I would have preferred at that moment for him to be running around, too," Jessie said. "But looking back, this is when I saw the first instance of that self-control, this discipline, and not only that, this desire to do the right thing and not follow the crowd. He learned all that so early."

If those traits would later serve him well, Perry didn't need to look far to see another example of a pioneer in action. It was his dad, Perry Sr., who, despite long odds, was making a living in the field of building construction with his own brick-cleaning business. For years, the Wallace kids called it "Daddy's business in a bucket." Perry Sr. had no car when he first got started, so each morning he would load his steel brushes and acid into his bucket and ride the city bus to jobs all over town. Eventually, as business improved, he was able to buy a car, which allowed him to work jobs as far away as southern Kentucky and northern Alabama. This at a time when merely pulling over for gas was a risky proposition for a black man in the South.

As Perry Sr. began to make a little money, he saw an opportunity to improve his family's lot. Boxes were packed, and Short 26th was home no more; the family moved to a bigger, nicer house at 1110 Cass Street. The all-white North High School was right across the street, but the neighborhood was becoming increasingly black as whites moved to the suburbs.

It was around this time that young Perry's view of the world and its possibilities began to expand. He was now living at the edges of the cocoon of black life, near the divide between the white neighborhoods and the black neighborhoods, and old enough to notice the difference between the ways other people lived versus his own poor environment. His mother, who worked as a cleaning lady in office buildings downtown, brought home magazines she found in the trash. Perry was fascinated by the photos that depicted a world he did not know. And then he found another way to peek into this other world—literally. He could see the white students walking to and from North High School across the street, and on Friday nights in the fall, there were the football games.

Perry and his buddies would walk over to Robertson's corner store and buy some Cokes and cheese and bologna and crackers, and then make their way over to the chain-link fence that sat atop a hill overlooking the football field. Invisible to the crowd below, they stood at the edge of the fence and watched the spectacle at the white school—one that black people were prohibited from seeing any other way. As they peeked through the chains, Wallace later concluded, he and his friends were in effect looking through what the famous civil rights activist W. E. B. Du Bois called the "veil that separates the races."

"We stood there on Friday nights and we watched the games, but we also watched the people," Wallace recalled. "We watched whites live and enjoy being an American. They had popcorn and candy and a band and cheerleaders and hot dogs, and it just looked like they had a better place than we did. And I think the subtle signal that was sent was that even though they were poor, they were better than we were and they were more a part of the real America than we were."

Perry became interested in finding other ways to escape the rigid boundaries society had placed around him. The family's black-and-white television (this was before the days of color TVs!) brought a new world into their home, with Perry watching the popular shows of the day like *Leave It to Beaver* and *The Dick Van Dyke Show*, programs that depicted an image of the American middle class that intrigued him.

But the reality of life in Nashville was far different than it was on TV. When the first black students arrived at previously all-white schools on September 9, 1957, they were greeted by a crowd of angry white people hurling insults and rocks. Later that night, an entire wing of a Nashville elementary school was destroyed by a dynamite blast.

In the midst of this dangerous atmosphere, Perry Wallace, an asthmatic kid who had been taught by his parents to stay out of trouble, had to walk to school. And to get there, on his way to Elliott Elementary, he had to walk through white neighborhoods, past white schools.

Sometimes the white boys threw rocks at him. Sometimes they called him names. Sometimes a carload of teens sped by, throwing things *and* calling him names. And at least one group of punks surrounded him and threatened him with a knife. In those moments, Wallace later recalled, he "had to figure out the basic law of the jungle. It was fight or flight. It was classic and it was raw." Sometimes he fought; sometimes he ran. Sometimes he took the bus, just to avoid the bullies.

But even that plan didn't always work. Nearly fifty years later, Wallace vividly remembered one incident. Late on a spring afternoon, he stood alone on a street corner, waiting for a bus home.

A car packed with white boys rolled down the road toward him, the teens shouting insults as they approached. Perry stood his ground, waiting for the car to pass by. But as the car came closer, one of the guys leaned out and pointed a gun right at him. Time seemed to slow down, the shouts now just so much white noise, and Perry's eyes grew large as he stared down the barrel of the gun. The car slowed to a crawl as it turned the corner in front of him, and the guy just kept pointing the gun at Perry—pointing it, pointing it, pointing it—everything in slow motion. And then he didn't shoot.

"Maybe they were just kidding, because people just didn't

As an elementary school student in Nashville, Perry Wallace was often confronted by young white kids on his way to school.

COURTESY OF PERRY WALLACE.

shoot people in Nashville in those days," Wallace said. "But who knew? Who knew?"

Faced with no easy solution—ride the bus or walk, it made no difference; trouble could lurk anywhere—Perry lost himself in other pursuits. He found comfort in attending church, ignoring the taunts of the neighbor kids as he clutched his Bible. And he came to love music. Perry's father surprised him one day in fifth grade by bringing home a trumpet. Though Perry was never told exactly why he received the gift, he later got the sense that his father wanted him to enjoy the benefits of the study of music, that it would serve as a safe way to help him forget his troubles and escape to new worlds.

Perry's love for the trumpet continued as he graduated from the Elliott School and enrolled at Wharton Junior High. Almost immediately, Perry noticed one comforting advantage to attending Wharton: the walk to school was peaceful. While the journey to Elliott had taken him through white areas, the walk to Wharton took him in the opposite direction, closer to all-black universities like Fisk and Tennessee A&I and deeper into the heart of black Nashville.

As the scenery changed, so, too, did Wallace's curiosities. The year was 1960, and Nashville was the stage for some of the first dramatic scenes of the civil rights movement. In February of that year, local college students staged peaceful sit-ins at Nashville's department-store lunch counters, protesting the fact that blacks were not allowed to eat there. Though angry whites beat them and burned cigarettes into their flesh, these students remained true to the teachings of nonviolence and didn't respond by fighting back.

For Wallace, it was the beginning of an education unlike anything he had ever imagined. Why did he have to use a *different* water fountain downtown? Why did he have to sit in the *back* of the bus? The more curious he became about these questions, the more he had to see what these older students were doing at the protests. He and some friends would sneak downtown—their parents would *kill* them if they knew what they were up to—and watch the action at the department stores and cafeterias from a safe distance.

His thirst for knowledge was intense. After school and on weekends, he walked a few miles to the Hadley Park library and buried himself in the works of the civil rights leader W. E. B. Du Bois, and absorbed the accounts of Southern lynchings written by another prominent black writer and activist, Walter White.

There was no hanging out at the fast-food joint after school, no detours on the way home from band practice. While other guys in the neighborhood developed their own signature swaggering struts, that wasn't an option for Perry: "Daddy said, 'You can't have a cool walk. Cool walk? That's out.'"

To keep the kids out of trouble, the Wallace parents kept

their kids in the house. The Wallace kids even *sounded* different from their peers, and that was no accident. They were taunted for this, too, told they were trying to sound white.

"The notion was not trying to be white; that was the last thing you wanted to be," Wallace recalled. "It was, what works in America now, and what is going to work in the future? We were living in a very humble place where people up and down the street talked and acted a whole different way. And what we understood was that these people were locking themselves in, potentially in a perilous and maybe even tragic way. So you understood what you needed to do, and you took the hits. People would give you hell, and you always would have doubts. But this was a decision I thought made a lot of sense and would pay off."

Perry Wallace made a conscious effort to be different from the people around him. But in one very important way, he fit in just fine.

When Perry stepped onto a basketball court, he was just one of the guys.

Chapter 3

Freedom Song

"Do you know how to dribble a basketball?"

In the chain of events that would come to define Perry Wallace's life, all the tragic and heroic moments, it was this simple question from his cousin Clarence that set everything in motion.

Around ten years old, Perry answered, no, he never had dribbled a basketball. He didn't even *have* a basketball.

With his brother, James, off in the air force, Perry found his older cousin an intriguing role model. If Clarence, so athletic and smart, thought playing basketball was a good thing, then it must be true.

Perry's protective parents allowed Clarence to take Perry across the street to the playground at North High School—

when the white kids weren't around—to teach him how to play. On long summer nights, Clarence taught his younger cousin the fundamentals: Dribbling. Shooting. Rebounding. His pupil—the trumpet-playing, Sunday-school-teaching voracious reader—loved every minute of it.

"I caught the bug," Wallace remembers, "and things took off from there."

Perry began spending more time at the North High hoops, learning the game from older kids who cut him no slack. The late bloomer excelled.

It was at this same time that Perry found a new outlet for his imagination. He could look around town and admire the basketball players at all-black high schools and colleges like Pearl High and Tennessee A&I, young men who not only were succeeding in a segregated society, but whose talents were recognized and celebrated. And he could turn on the television and see black role models of a different sort, NBA legends like Wilt Chamberlain, Bill Russell, and Oscar Robertson.

"It was so spectacular to see them out in a world where they were in the mainstream. And what we knew about the mainstream at the time was that we weren't allowed to be in it," Wallace recalled. "To see these guys have their strength and artistry respected in the larger world was huge. They were the ones you tried to be like."

And then, heaven. Wilt Chamberlain and his Philadelphia

Warriors came to Nashville to play an exhibition game at Tennessee A&I. Somehow, Perry got permission from his parents to go to the game. There, decked out in the blue and gold of the Warriors, was the "Big Dipper": huge (seven foot one), charismatic, and dunking like crazy.

"To actually see Chamberlain, this had such an impact on me, it's hard to describe," Wallace said.

Some kids in the neighborhood wished they could fly through the air. Others dreamed of making themselves invisible or as fast as lightning. The only superpower Perry Wallace wanted was to dunk a basketball like Chamberlain. Never mind that Wilt was virtually without peer in those days, as rare a sight as any caped crusader. Perry had a plan.

Every night, after finishing dinner and homework, he made his way to the living room, took a spot in front of the family's TV, and got down to business. He knew he had to strengthen his skinny legs if he wanted to jump high enough to dunk, so he improvised a workout routine. One. Ten. Fifty. One hundred. Who knows how many squats he did in that living room, bending at the knees over and over again, his eyes on the TV and his sights on the prize, that rim that loomed ten feet off the ground on every backboard in town.

As his legs grew stronger, he tested himself on the baskets at North High. From age ten to age twelve, he was a fixture on those courts.

"The dog's baying at the moon, I'm jumping at the goal," he recalled. "I tried and tried and tried, and then one summer, I had to be twelve years old, I finally dunked the ball." Literally and figuratively, he had reached a goal. And with that fulfillment came success on two important fronts.

One, he gained respect from the same kids who mocked his studiousness. "In some respects, our enthusiasm for the game was what we had in common, and the dunk was the high point of that," Wallace said. "Otherwise, I would have been a very different, strange little kid playing the trumpet four or five hours a day and listening to classical music when everybody else was listening to Motown. On the court, we all came together and we were just the same."

Two, he found in basketball a passage to freedom and accomplishment in a society structured to limit both for black children. "Playground basketball allowed a sense of expression in a world that was dark and uncertain and in which there were a lot of ways that you were weak," he said. "This, on the other hand, was bright. You could express all these different things, this artistry. It was like a big lift, and the dunk was like a freedom song."

As Wallace's abilities improved, he began playing pickup games with college players from A&I. "The older guys were amazed," Wallace recalled. "I was running around playing full-court basketball. They'd say, 'Look at this young boy dunk!'"

Just as he had done on the playground at North High, he was playing ball against older kids. They were a big influence.

And then, one day, David Lattin strolled into the gym.

Bye-bye, old influences. Hello, Big Daddy D.

In three years, Lattin would lead an unheard-of college named Texas Western to the NCAA championship, part of an all-black starting five that would pull off a huge upset, startling legendary coach Adolph Rupp and his Kentucky Wildcats in the 1966 title game, and serve notice to a national television audience that the days of all-white basketball were over. But for now, Lattin was about to enroll at A&I. He wouldn't last a semester in Nashville before transferring to Texas Western and making history, but none of that mattered now. He was "big, strong, and menacing," Wallace recalled. The baddest man in the gym.

Wallace, of course, could dunk. The guys he played with at A&I could dunk. He had watched Chamberlain and Russell dunk. All these guys would pull out the occasional in-your-face slam, but in that era, most dunks were still quick little stuffs, more about efficiency than theater. But Lattin took the dunk to another level.

"Guys played very serious ball, everybody's sweating and going after it," Wallace said, "but [Lattin] would get the ball and go down the floor and he would do the Michael Jordan dunk—his legs were spread apart the same way—and he'd be flying through the air and everybody under the basket went, 'Time to leave, time to go, don't even mess with this, get out of the way!' He's so far in another league, it had a big impression on me."

Hard as it is to believe now, when basketball phenoms seemingly have signed lifetime sneaker contracts and reality-show TV deals by the time they reach puberty, Wallace, who was nearing the end of ninth grade, had not yet been contacted by the highly respected Pearl High basketball coach Cornelius Ridley. Wallace wasn't surprised. He wasn't angry. He just thought he wasn't going to be on the team.

The truth was, yes, the guy who could dunk since the time he was twelve, who wanted to be just like Wilt Chamberlain, who held his own in games against college players, yes, that kid would be going to Pearl.

With the full intention of trying out for the band.

And not the basketball team.

His junior high band teacher had already made a connection with the Pearl band director. The road to the marching band was paved. But there was no clear path to the basketball team.

"Unfortunately, that's how a lot of things happen in life," Wallace would say of his basketball career that nearly never was. "I was just going to go in the band, and that seemed fine. I liked basketball, I loved it, but I didn't have the sense that I could do any more with it. I didn't have a sense of how you make that connection to the team at Pearl. Do they talk to you? Do you talk to them? What do you do? It was clearer with the band."

Coming off a 1963 national championship, Ridley had lost a number of key players and was looking to reload his team. Ridley had seen Wallace play, but Perry wasn't at the top of his mind when he paid a visit to A&I coach Harold Hunter early in the fall.

"Have you seen the Wallace kid?" Hunter asked.

"You mean the big kid in the band?" Ridley replied.

"The band?! Have you seen the boy dunk?!"

One can only imagine that it was with Road Runner–like speed that Ridley vacated Coach Hunter's office and emerged at Hattie Wallace's dinner table. The coach knocked on the door at Cass Street, intent on pulling the six-foot-five incoming sophomore out of the trumpet section and onto his basketball team.

As Ridley put on his best recruiting pitch, Mr. and Mrs. Wallace worried about Perry's schoolwork, about bad influences, about the lessons they had worked so hard to teach him.

Perry thought about actually being one of those Pearl High Tigers he looked up to, about playing ball in the old gym, which was so raucous on game nights. He had thought he just wanted to be in the band, but the more Ridley talked, the more Wallace realized what he really wanted to do. Perry Sr. could sense it.

"You've got to keep your grades up," father told son. "You've got to act like you have some sense, you've got to respect people, and you've got to keep going to church. If you do all those, all the time, you can play [basketball]. Otherwise, come back home."

Chapter 4

Pearl of the Community

PERRY WALLACE SAYS THAT ONE of the proudest days of his life was the bright, sunny morning in September 1963 when he walked through the doors of Pearl High School on his first day as a Pearl student.

It was a powerful moment for many reasons. His brother and sisters had gone to Pearl. He was fascinated by the basketball team and the band. He admired the smart and confident Pearl students he saw around the neighborhood. He loved Pearl long before he ever experienced it for himself, as if the school were already a part of his very being.

In a way, it was. When he walked through those doors, he followed in the footsteps of generations. A Pearl education was something just about every black person who grew up in

Nashville had in common. Class pictures dating back to the 1890s lined the walls of each corridor, and it seemed as if the eyes in the photos were staring through the souls of the students who walked down the halls, encouraging them to build on the sacrifices of preceding generations. The school wasn't just the pride of the neighborhood in the 1960s; it had been that centerpiece for more than eighty years.

Pearl was a classic example of one of the ironies of segregation. The same forces designed to limit blacks—most significantly in terms of jobs and neighborhoods—created just the environment necessary for these jewels of education to emerge. With limited job opportunities, many of the most talented black college graduates became teachers. With only a few high schools—or in many cases, just one—available to black students, the best and brightest kids weren't scattered across many schools; they shared the same classrooms. With blacks confined to tightly defined neighborhoods—the cocoon—these schools naturally became hugely important community institutions, an extension of church and family.

"A lot of our parents were not educated people, but they knew the value of education and the doors it could open for you," said Pearl alum Lee Hayden. "Going to Pearl was a great opportunity, and we shouldn't be squandering it whatsoever. Not graduating from high school was not an option, even if it took you four hundred years."

Pearl teachers knew the odds were stacked against their students, but they also understood that the world was changing, that opportunities would be available to these kids that they never enjoyed themselves. Wallace's Class of '66 entered Pearl as sophomores just a week after Martin Luther King's famous "I Have a Dream" speech in 1963. Before he and his classmates earned their diplomas, they'd see the passage of the 1964 Civil Rights Act, which made it illegal to discriminate based on race, skin color, religion, or gender, and the 1965 Voting Rights Act, a law that outlawed racial discrimination related to voting in elections.

America, it seemed, was opening its doors, and this generation of students would enter adulthood at just the right time. "There was something special in the air," Wallace recalled. "Perhaps it was hope, maybe it was just a sense of excitement. But by then even those of us who were not directly involved in civil rights activity could tell there was movement and change on the racial front."

Embracing their roles as mentors at this critical point in history, Pearl's teachers threw themselves into their jobs with uncommon enthusiasm and dedication, and in the process created a rich, nurturing, and intellectual environment that made up for the deficits of a separate and unequal system. Decades later, Perry Wallace coined a term for it: Pearl had become separate but *equalized*.

The special danger of separate but unequal was the message sent to black kids that they were inferior. *Separate but equalized,* Wallace came to believe, was the most positive response possible to the discriminatory practices of a separate and unequal world.

To create an *equalized* environment, Pearl teachers spent their own money to buy new textbooks to replace the tattered ones sent over from white high schools. They made sure black celebrities passing through Nashville took some time to inspire the students. They talked about equality and opportunity, and taught lessons about black history that could be found in no textbook.

"Our teachers invested in us day after day, made us set high standards, and held us to them," Wallace said. "Opportunity seemed so close at hand. Things were happening right before our eyes, and there seemed to be such a good possibility of people living really good lives."

Students gravitated toward Minerva Hawkins, a history teacher who was such a captivating speaker that some students spent their free periods or homeroom hours sitting in on extra lectures. An expert on African American history, Hawkins made sure her students were aware of the contributions of blacks that were so often ignored. "That's what the textbooks tell us," Hawkins would say, closing her book. "Now let me tell you what really happened."

Wallace was especially influenced by trigonometry teacher Dorothy Crippens. Short, petite, prim, and proper, Crippens had taught Perry's sisters years earlier, and because she saw such promise in their younger brother, she pushed Wallace hard. He loved the challenge.

"Our teachers made us feel special," said Wallace's former Pearl classmate and friend Donna Murray. "In an unspoken way, they made us know that we were somebody, that nobody could tell us we were less than that."

Years later, Wallace came to better understand the lasting impact of those student-teacher relationships. He thought about the battles his teachers must have fought to earn their degrees, the pain and frustration of emerging educated into a world of closed doors and scarce opportunities.

"Our teachers somehow took all this insult, this institutionalized, nationalized insult called segregation, and turned it into a force to make the world better, and particularly to do it through all these young students," Wallace said. "Sometimes they seemed a little mean and to have an edge. I guess I can understand that now. This was the America they lived in; for all the good, there was all this madness."

Chapter 5

The Woomp Show

WOOOOOOOOMP! Woooooomp! Woooooooooomp!

Sometimes being a student at Pearl was just plain fun. There was nothing more exhilarating than the "woomp show" before a basketball game in the old gym.

Here came the Pearl High players in their satin warm-up suits, red and white pinstripes and Tigers team logo ablaze. The gym was already packed, and it was only halftime of the JV game when the varsity players came running out on the court for their early warm-ups, accompanied by "Sweet Georgia Brown," theme song of the Harlem Globetrotters.

Balls bouncing, sneakers squeaking, girls shrieking.

First some layups, Tiger after Tiger rolling to the hoop and laying the ball off the glass.

The repetition was hypnotic, Tiger after Tiger, but then there was a wink, and *woooomp!*—there it was, Willie Fisher flew through the air and dunked the ball. And then another guard, Joe Herbert, dunked it, and then came Hound McClain, and the crowd yelled, *"Woooomp!"*—another dunk. And then came the forwards and centers, and the dunks got more powerful and the *wooomps* got louder. *Wooomp! Wooomp! Woooomp!*

And then to finish it all off, to make the walls shake and the gym cave in, came the high-flyingest dunker of them all. Here came Perry Wallace with a swish-swash reverse slam or a tomahawk or a rock-the-cradle or a one-handed windmill to top it all off, and the gym erupted with one final *woooomp!*

The dunk was Perry's "freedom song" and his connection to his classmates, and it was also the end—before the game had even begun—for more than a few Pearl opponents, who stood on the other end of the court, slack-jawed, watching an entire team dunk the ball in warm-ups. *Woooomp!* Game over.

Some coaches frowned upon such displays of individual flair, but not Cornelius Ridley. The Pearl coach knew the demoralizing effect the dunks had on his opponents, and he encouraged his players to throw them down with authority.

As a biology teacher, Ridley intimidated some of his students, never allowing any joking or horseplay in his classroom. On the practice court, he demanded complete respect. Many

Pearl players believed that their practices were harder than their games, but because they knew Ridley had won multiple championships, they bought into his hard-driving style without complaint. Ridley began each session with individual drills, designed to improve skills such as ball handling. The players worked against each other two-on-two or three-on-three before the whole team practiced together, running through specific plays. He ran the same sets over and over until his guys got it right. All the while, Ridley was thoroughly engaged, pouring his soul into the workouts.

Ridley's zeal in practice, however, was nothing compared to his energetic demeanor in games. In particularly intense games, one of the primary duties for Assistant Coach James Armstrong was to hold him back from the referees while shouting, "Calm down, Ridley, calm down!" pulling and yanking on him like a deckhand trying to keep a man from falling overboard in a heavy sea.

Ridley was energetic, for sure, but he was also a student of the game and an insightful reader of people, knowing exactly which buttons to push at any given time. Ridley's style was unlike anything Perry Wallace had ever experienced. The coach was demanding and he was out of control at times, but Perry loved him.

Ridley's intensity had a huge effect on Wallace, helping draw the naïve kid out of his shell. Many times, Ridley and his wife would drive Perry home after games. The coach would engage his young ballplayer in conversations on all sorts of subjects, sharing his thoughts on people, on the times, and on the ways of the world. Driving through the streets of North Nashville on those dark winter nights, a deep friendship developed between the coach and the "shy little boy who was afraid of [his] own shadow." It was as if Ridley were injecting the book-smart Wallace with booster shots of street smarts and perspective.

"What I learned from him were things that were just not a part of me at the time," Wallace says. "He knew people and he knew the world so very well, and I didn't. I was the good little boy who was naïve and didn't hang out on the streets or go to parties, so I didn't know a lot of 'grown-up' stuff. But Ridley had so much savvy and he helped me develop a deeper knowledge of people and life."

Over the years, Wallace would build on the lessons taught by Ridley and become known as someone with an uncommonly insightful perspective on people and events—a fact, he said, that would have shocked those who grew up around him.

Chapter 6

Not Just Another Game

TOGETHER, THE WISE COACH AND the willing student made a dynamic pair. Along with a roster full of players who would go on to play college ball, Wallace would be a part of a state championship team in Tennessee's all-black league in the 1964 season, his first at Pearl.

At this time, the state's high school sports associations were still segregated—black schools played in one tournament, while white schools played in another. But change was coming.

Black schools would participate only as "affiliate members" of the Tennessee Secondary School Athletic Association in 1965, meaning they would compete in an all-black subset of the TSSAA before becoming eligible for unified state championships in 1966.

While the public schools plodded along gradually toward integrating black and white players, Nashville's private Father Ryan High School forged a different path. First, the Catholic school scheduled football games against integrated teams from Kentucky. Then, nearly a decade after admitting its first black students, Father Ryan finally allowed some of those boys to participate on its athletic teams beginning in the 1963–64 school year. When the Irish basketball team picture was taken that year, there were two black faces in it, belonging to Willie Brown and Jesse Porter.

And then Ryan coach Bill Derrick got an idea. It was one thing for his integrated team to play against Nashville's all-white competition. How about testing his talented team against the very best? How about playing Pearl?

The moment Coach Derrick picked up the phone and called Cornelius Ridley, the idea of an all-black Tennessee high school playing basketball against a mostly white team went from unthinkable to inevitable.

No sooner had the two coaches scheduled the South's first game between a black and a predominantly white school—for January 4, 1965—than it became the most highly anticipated basketball game in Nashville history. As players and coaches from both teams enjoyed the Christmas holiday, they were bombarded with questions from friends and neighbors. Tony Moorman, a Pearl forward, couldn't escape the hype anywhere. Even at church, all anyone wanted to talk about was the Ryan game.

All this was taking place during one of the most intense periods of the civil rights movement. Just a year and a half earlier, the 16th Street Baptist Church in Birmingham, Alabama, had been bombed, killing four young black girls; six months earlier, President Johnson had signed the Civil Rights Act; five months earlier, civil rights workers—one black, two white—were killed by Ku Klux Klan members in Mississippi. One month after the game, Malcolm X would be shot down in New York; two months later, Selma, Alabama, would be the site of police attacks on peaceful protestors; seven months later, President Lyndon Johnson would sign the Voting Rights Act, and racially charged riots in the Watts section of Los Angeles would set the city ablaze.

Interest in the game was so overwhelming that both schools realized that neither of their own gyms would be large enough to accommodate the crowd. Neither would Vanderbilt's Memorial Gym, which had a capacity of 7,229. The game, then, would be played downtown at Municipal Auditorium, the city's largest arena.

"We understood," Wallace recalled, "that this was not just another game."

January 4, 1965. Game day.

In Washington, D.C., President Johnson delivered his State

of the Union address, talking to the nation about a "Great Society," an iconic agenda that spawned programs to improve public health, protect the environment, fight poverty, support the arts, and combat racism.

In downtown Nashville, Memphis attorney A. W. Willis Jr. walked into the state capitol and took his seat at a rickety old desk, becoming the first black person since Reconstruction to serve in the Tennessee General Assembly.

And just a few blocks away at Municipal Auditorium, the gates to history opened at 6:00 p.m., fans from both schools flooding into the arena with their $1.25 general admission tickets, so many of them coming in so fast that the doors were locked before tip-off.

As usual, Pearl's varsity squad put on its high-flying "woomp show" during halftime of the JV game, nearly sending Ryan varsity center Robert Forte, who had poked his head out of the locker room to see what the noise was all about, into cardiac arrest when he mistook the Pearl varsity for the JV.

"I thought if this is the B team, we don't have a chance," Forte said.

Both junior varsity teams played tight with so many eyes watching their every move, but the Pearl JVs ended up winning the game handily.

After brief remarks by the principals of both schools, it was time for the main event, the first of sixty-three varsity high school basketball games in Nashville that week but the only one that truly mattered.

Once again, Wallace and his teammates went through their dunking show in pregame warm-ups. Dunk. *Woomp!* Dunk. *Woomp!* Father Ryan guard Pat Sanders found himself momentarily mesmerized by a sight he'd never seen on a basketball court as the Pearl players (every single one of them!) rolled to the basket and threw down dunk after dunk. Father Ryan coach Derrick, seeing that the Tiger routine was having its desired effect, yelled at Sanders to either quit staring or head back to the locker room.

The game started, and most fans remained standing, as they would for the entire game. The crowd was so loud that at one point in the first quarter, Father Ryan was issued a technical foul when Coach Derrick couldn't hear the buzzer summoning the team back to the court after a time-out.

Though his team held a slight height advantage over Pearl, Coach Derrick believed the Tigers' strength and leaping ability would prevent his team from collecting many rebounds, especially on the offensive end. *We're only going to get one shot each time down the court,* he thought, *so we better make it count.* Father Ryan took its time, working the ball around and waiting for the perfect shot.

The deliberate style worked, with Ryan holding a 15–11 lead after the first period. In the second quarter, Pearl's speed and pressure altered the flow of the game, and Wallace began to dominate. He hit five of seven shots, sending the Pearl crowd into pandemonium with two dunks, one off a fast break and the other following a missed free throw.

Pearl led 31–29 at halftime and scored the first six points of the third quarter to take an eight-point advantage.

Cue Willie Brown.

One of three black players on the Father Ryan roster but the only one to play in the game, Brown grew up in the same neighborhood as many of the Pearl players. All the Tigers knew him; they had played with him in summer pickup games for years. His girlfriend was even a Pearl High cheerleader! In many ways, for the one time in his career, Brown was the most comfortable guy on the court. Half the crowd was rooting for his team; the other half—and all his opponents—knew him and admired him.

Brown hit a shot. And another. And another. And another. He added a free throw. As the fourth quarter began, he had pulled the Irish to within one point, down 44–43. The pace of the game slowed considerably, both teams trading baskets until Ron Parham put Pearl up 51–50 with just thirty-six seconds remaining.

And then, a blur.

After Parham's basket, Pearl gets the ball back but almost immediately turns it right back over to Father Ryan. The final seconds tick away, all the fans standing and cheering, everyone knowing the ball is headed in Willie Brown's direction, and it is, and he shoots from the right corner, but the ball caroms off the rim, and it looks as if Pearl has won!

But there is Father Ryan's Lyn Dempsey, the backup guard who hasn't scored a point or grabbed a rebound all game, and the ball lands in his hands, and he takes a step back, and Wallace lunges toward him, and Dempsey launches the ball high over the defender's arms, and the buzzer sounds, and the ball soars fifteen feet before it rips through the net . . . and Ryan has won, 52–51.

Dempsey was the hero, but the star of the game, this first-ever contest between black and white, was the black player on the mostly white team named Brown, Willie Brown, whose twenty-one points led all scorers.

Those hoping the game would strike a blow for racial reconciliation couldn't have asked for more. Far from being awkward or unnatural or unfair or whatever else segregationists thought might happen if white kids and black kids stepped on the court together, this game had been so well played that one fan leaving the arena was heard to say that fans should have to pay another $1.25 to get out. A black player had excelled on an integrated team, one of the most high-profile examples in Nashville's history of blacks and whites working together to achieve a common goal. All this was a step in the right direction, something many of the Pearl players would admit decades later.

But for now, as they trudged off the court, the Tigers just felt numb.

Ever since this game had been announced, folks had approached them in the barbershops and in church and told them that this was the opportunity everyone in Nashville's black community had been waiting for, the first chance to compete on the same basketball court as whites and prove that blacks were just as good, if not better. You get that opportunity, the older folks told the Pearl players, and you play like there's no tomorrow.

They had done just that, but all that mattered was that they had lost. Perry Wallace and teammates Walter Fisher and Ted McClain walked off that court together, heads hanging low, feeling like they'd missed their chance to make history. And then, determined that he'd never feel this pain again as long as he wore a Pearl High uniform, McClain broke the silence.

"Walt," he said to Fisher, "you know, we ain't going to lose any more games."

They walked on, and Wallace lifted his head. "I don't think we will, either."

Chapter 7

They Had the Wrong Guy

THE PEARL HIGH TEAMMATES WERE proven wrong almost immediately, losing another game eleven days later. But after that, the Tigers completed the rest of Wallace's junior season without another defeat, eventually winning the final all-black state tournament championship in Tennessee history.

The following season, they would compete against white schools as full members of the TSSAA. When they'd lost to Father Ryan, it had seemed as though they'd let their one and only opportunity to prove themselves slip by. Now, thanks to the mergers of the black and white athletic associations, they'd have another chance. But it wouldn't be as simple as just winning one game against an integrated team. To make a statement that mattered, they would have to win the 1966 state championship.

"Our senior season was going to be the culmination of everything we had worked for all our lives," Wallace recalled. "Coach Ridley talked about it—not too much, but enough. But apart from that, we knew. Even though there was turmoil in America, there were coming to be more openings and opportunities for blacks, and we felt the energy of that."

Losing to Father Ryan, Wallace came to believe, was the best thing that ever happened to Pearl. The players felt they had let not only themselves down, but also the entire black community. In practice sessions during the ramp-up to their senior year and throughout that season, Wallace said, the Tigers played with a ferocity that was "even greater than it would have been otherwise. We were good—we played hard and we played tough—but there was even more to it."

Pearl's winning streak dating back to the 1965 season kept growing: thirteen, twenty-three, thirty-three games in a row overall; twenty-one wins and no losses for the 1966 regular season. The Tigers were so good that virtually every player attracted interest from college recruiters, with eight members of the team going on to play college ball. But it was Perry Wallace, surely one of the only valedictorians in the country who could also dunk and average nineteen rebounds a game, who received the most attention.

By this time, Perry Sr.'s brick-cleaning business was doing well enough that the family had purchased their own home for the first time, and the mailbox at the white house at 1908 Tenth Avenue became flooded with letters from college coaches from all over the country. Soon the coaches themselves started arriving at the doorstep to talk to Perry and his parents, so many coming so often with such great things to say about their son that Mrs. Wallace told her daughter Jessie, "I do believe that President Lyndon B. Johnson will step on this porch one day, because everybody wants our boy!"

Any recruiter interested in Perry Wallace wouldn't just have to go through his parents; they'd have to deal with Cornelius Ridley, too.

"I remember hearing Ridley, at the end of practice, telling Perry to come by his office, which was in the locker room," Perry's teammate Tony Moorman recalled. "We would be dressing after practice, and I would listen to Ridley. 'Iowa came in today, Iowa State came in, two or three others came in.' And then I'd turn to the others and say, 'Man, Perry got four more offers!'"

From the time that Wallace first began to understand that he might be able to earn a college basketball scholarship, he told his coach exactly what he was looking for.

"I told him I loved the game and what I wanted to do

was to get a scholarship to a good university," Wallace said. All through the process, Ridley repeated a simple phrase to his young star: "Make the right choice," he implored Perry, "make the right choice."

Initially, Wallace was certain that the right choice would mean leaving the stifling segregation of the South. A basketball scholarship would provide the opportunity to realize a dream. From the time he'd started reading those magazines his mother had brought home from work, the ones that had shown Wallace a world outside of his hometown, one that he'd never known, he'd dedicated his life not only to preparing for the future but to getting out of Nashville.

"You had this feeling that you could be part of the larger world if you were in the North. The image was that you would have more opportunities and not the harsh prejudices," Wallace recalled. "I saw myself moving up North, moving into the American middle class, getting a job maybe as an engineer, living in an integrated setting with a nice house and a nice family."

When letters arrived from Big Ten universities in the Midwest—schools such as Iowa, Wisconsin, Michigan, Northwestern, and Purdue—Wallace took notice. He would begin taking trips to visit some of the schools during the basketball season, others as soon as it ended. These were the first airplane flights of his life—heady stuff for a teenager, being flown all over the country and treated like the most important person in the world. On his recruiting visit to Iowa, Wallace arrived at the airport along with another basketball recruit and a football player. There to greet the trio was a marching band, which promptly whisked them away on a parade through Iowa City, culminating with a photo op with the governor.

Perry's visit to Northwestern was especially meaningful since his brother, James, was then living with his wife in the Chicago suburb of Evanston, where the school was located. Because of their age difference, Perry had never really gotten to know his older brother, but he could still recall the scent of Old Spice cologne on James's blue air force uniform from the times he'd hugged him good-bye back when Perry was a kid. When Perry visited the Northwestern campus, he brought James along, the younger brother feeling an immense satisfaction in seeing his older brother treated well by the people they encountered on campus.

Perry was thoroughly enjoying the recruiting process. But he also began to pick up on the dirty, unethical side of the recruiting game. The types of illegal offers that were quite attractive to the typical wide-eyed recruit were wasted on Wallace.

There was the cash—sometimes a promise of money if he signed with the school, sometimes a straight-out roll of two or three hundred dollars to "tide him over" for the weekend.

There were even bigger offers—"Here's a car, you ride around in it," he was told—and there were promises of fancier cars upon his arrival, maybe even a nice town house to live in.

"All of that was great, it was just that they had the wrong guy," Wallace said. "I really didn't care about that stuff. I had no interest in that and it really turned me off to the places that tried to make a deal with me. It seemed to me that there were a lot of good possibilities in life just by playing by the rules."

In their recruiting pitches, many coaches would throw in a bit of negative talk about schools in the South that were showing interest in Wallace, stressing the hardships he'd surely endure. It wasn't a point Wallace needed to be sold on: his whole goal was to get out of the South. The problem was, as great as that urge remained, it wasn't enough to blind him to the lives he saw many of the black student-athletes living on Northern campuses.

He wasn't going to trade one plantation for another.

As he saw it, the big, strong, talented black athletes were being asked to produce on the athletic fields and then retreat to their dorms until called upon again. It was pure exploitation.

"That rattled me. It scared me," Wallace recalled. "I'd talk to players, and it was obvious that they weren't getting a chance to think and develop socially and to take advantage of a great university and a rich social environment. My attitude was 'Wait a minute, what else is left? You're getting great basketball, but you're not doing great academics, and you're not really integrating and participating in this microcosm of American society, so why should I go there?'"

It was a mature—and upsetting—realization, but it opened the door for a school that was one of the unlikeliest destinations of all for a black kid from Short 26th: Vanderbilt University.

Chapter 8

The Name of the Game

WHEN VANDERBILT BASKETBALL COACH ROY Skinner climbed the twenty-four steps outside Kirkland Hall on his way to Chancellor Alexander Heard's office sometime in late 1963 or early 1964, he knew the conversation was going to have enormous consequences for his basketball program. It wasn't every day that he was invited to the chancellor's office; in fact, this was the first time. Yes, Skinner thought, the conversation was going to be important: he and the new chancellor would be talking about expanding the seating capacity of Memorial Gymnasium to accommodate the growing demand for tickets.

The chancellor and the coach discussed plans to add balconies to the north end of the gym, and then, almost casually, Heard floated an idea by his coach.

"He told me that Vanderbilt was open to blacks," Skinner recalled more than forty years later, "and he told me that I could recruit a black player and, in fact, that he would like for me to."

In his trademark low-key way, Skinner's reaction proved that changing the course of history need not require a confrontational first act. When challenged to do something that had never been done before in a conference whose member institutions spanned the former states of the Confederacy, he didn't come up with excuses, he didn't threaten to quit, he didn't appeal to an influential alum to try to change the chancellor's mind.

He simply said, "OK."

Skinner was an unlikely racial integrationist. The man Heard asked to take the historic step of recruiting the first black basketball player in the Southeastern Conference was a Kentucky farm boy, only about a decade removed from running a Virginia youth center and coaching a high school tennis team, a man who had never played alongside or coached a black player at any level.

For all those reasons, Skinner was the unlikeliest of trailblazers. But in another respect, it made all the sense in the world. He was chasing the number one spot, willing to do whatever it took to knock his home-state Kentucky Wildcats from their perch atop the SEC.

"I didn't care what color they were if they could win," Skinner said. "That's the name of the game."

Growing up, Perry Wallace never thought much about Vanderbilt University, even though it was located in his hometown of Nashville, Tennessee. Throughout most of his childhood, he wouldn't have been welcome there as a student since the school didn't admit black students until 1964, and as a basketball fan, he was far more interested in the teams at Pearl and Tennessee A&I. But as the choice of a college became an important consideration, Vanderbilt entered the picture. As Wallace began to earn notice on the court and in the classroom, folks from Vanderbilt started to show up at the Pearl High gym. All his life, the message Wallace had heard from white Nashville was "You stay over there." Now, suddenly, people were coming over to his side of town to see him, and they were saying, "Come on and join us."

By the time Coach Skinner arrived at the Wallace home to pay a visit in the midst of what remained an undefeated season for Pearl, Perry had narrowed down offers from more than one hundred schools to just a handful. He'd even turned down a scholarship offer from UCLA, a program in the early stages of its historic run of ten NCAA championships in twelve years, because he felt he would have trouble earning significant playing time as a Bruin. Here was Skinner, about to try to persuade Wallace, a kid smart enough to see what was going on at the basketball factories up North and grounded enough to know he wasn't good enough to play at UCLA, to integrate the SEC. To make history—at a great cost. It should have been a tough sell.

But from the moment Skinner walked in the door, there was something all the Wallaces liked about him.

"My parents knew people, and they knew life," Wallace told author Frye Gaillard years later. "And they had a feeling about Coach Skinner. When he came over that day and sat down in our house, he had a certain manner about him, a certain honesty and decency, a rhythm and a style that seemed easygoing. My parents, of course, were looking at him hard. They were asking themselves, 'Who is this man who wants to take our son into dangerous territory?'"

Perry was listening to the coach through ears as skeptical as those of his parents. He heard something, however, that meant a lot back in 1966 and led him to take a closer look at Vanderbilt. When Skinner talked to his parents, he addressed them not by their first names, as would have been the convention of the day for a white man addressing blacks, but rather as Mr. and Mrs. Wallace. For Perry, eager for his parents to be treated with respect and looking for signals on how this Southern white coach might treat a black player, Skinner's choice of words spoke volumes.

"Coach Skinner treated me and my parents in a way that a lot of people back then would not have," Wallace said. "At that point, along with the comparison to those other schools that were recruiting me, I began to take Vanderbilt seriously."

For his part, Skinner's demeanor with the Wallaces was genuine; he was the same man in their home as he was in the company of any white family, a fact that was significant in its own right in 1966 Nashville. "I just called *all* parents Mister and Missus," he recalled, "especially since most of them were older than I was."

Even as the Pearl basketball season rolled along, Wallace attended games at Memorial Gym, spending time with the Commodore players to get a better sense of his potential future teammates and the lives they lived on campus. He was impressed by what he saw. Here was a place that offered the best of both worlds: big-time basketball and first-rate academics. Vanderbilt's engineering school had a fine reputation; there was little talk of the social life on campus, but Wallace wasn't much of a partier anyway. Star Commodore basketball player Clyde Lee walked him around the perimeter of the campus and showed him where the closest

Church of Christ chapel was located, a church Lee himself attended. There was not even a hint of scandal, no cash to tide him over on his drive back to North Nashville, no loaner cars to get him there.

Everything about Vanderbilt was appealing, except for one thing.

Perry Wallace did not want to be the first black basketball player in the Southeastern Conference; he had absolutely no interest in being a pioneer. If progress was going to happen, that was great, but not on his back.

What kind of crazy person would choose to step into the fire alone? With numbers came strength. There had been dozens of students at the sit-ins and Freedom Rides of the civil rights movement, thousands at the March on Washington, and millions watching it all on television. But to desegregate the SEC meant going it alone in backwater Southern towns filled with prejudiced people, a teenage black male sweeping through the South like a magnet, attracting all the scattered hatred left behind by the dangerous events of the mid-1960s.

As Wallace began to think deeply about whether this was a mission he wanted to accept, pressure mounted from all sides. His decision was entering the public realm; everyone in Nashville, it seemed, had an opinion on where Perry Wallace should attend college. What made a difficult choice even more complex were the mixed messages he received from both blacks and whites. Members of both camps urged him to make history at Vanderbilt; others from both sides were equally adamant that he go elsewhere.

Socially progressive white Vanderbilt alums expressed hope that he would break the color line at their school. Many blacks who believed in the promise of integration were also eager to see Wallace choose Vanderbilt. Positive as they were, these messages were accompanied by a corresponding pressure: the obligation to live up to high expectations.

And then there was the hate.

Perry's parents did their best to hide the mail that arrived at their home, and indeed their son didn't see most of the letters until years later. But some did slip past his parents' protective eyes, handwritten notes threatening Wallace's life if he made the choice to attend Vanderbilt.

Throughout it all, there was another source of information for Wallace. The most insightful people he heard from were the black neighbors, church parishioners, and family friends who held jobs as maids, waiters, shoe shiners, and cooks in the white community, people who were often invisible to those they served on the other side of town.

Listen to what I heard, they'd confide to Perry.

Some of them want you, some of them don't.

They're saying the team is doing just fine and they don't need to bring in a nigger.

They're saying a lot of Vanderbilt alums are rolling over in their graves right now, and some who are alive feel the same way.

Throughout the winter and early spring of 1966, Perry Wallace had a lot on his mind. So many people with opinions, so many big questions for a teenager to answer, so much pressure to make a decision.

The thing was, he really wasn't in any big hurry.

The Pearl Tigers still had a championship to win.

Chapter 9

Champions!

THE ONLY UNDEFEATED TEAM IN the 1966 state tournament, the Tigers felt enormous pressure to deliver a championship to Nashville's black community, their own small contribution to the civil rights gains taking place across the South.

To do so, they'd have to beat the talented team from Memphis's all-white Treadwell High School, a squad many considered to be the second-best team in the state.

This was going to be the championship game everyone wanted.

Mid-state against west-state.

Black against white for the title.

For the first time ever in Tennessee.

Like it or not, Perry Wallace and history seemed drawn to each other.

Alone in the Pearl locker room at Vanderbilt's Memorial Gym, the site of the state tournament, Coach Ridley took a moment to gather his thoughts as his players ran through their pregame dunkathon. Here it was, the opportunity he'd waited for his entire life.

But it wasn't enough just to win; Ridley believed the Tigers had to win in just the right way. Ever since Wallace and two teammates had busted a rim by dunking the ball in a regional game, Ridley had been more conscious than ever that his Tigers could make their greatest statement if they managed to win games while playing with a style that white fans could not possibly disparage as "wild black basketball." Ridley told his players that they didn't want to play out of control both for appearances' sake—everything they did reflected on the race—but also for the simple fact that if they slowed things down and minimized the chances to make mistakes, they could prove that blacks didn't choke when the stakes were high.

"People who only see you in terms of stereotypes have no idea that you're sitting down saying, 'We know what people think, so how are we going to proceed so that we can be effective and disabuse them of those thoughts?'" Wallace said. "They never stop and think that the people they're watching out on the court might have thought really, really hard about all that."

When his players returned to the locker room after their warm-up act, Ridley was ready to speak. All eyes were on him.

"You're not only representing Pearl High School," he told his players, "you're representing North Nashville, you're representing your household, and just about every black face in the state of Tennessee—you're representing them, too. You need to go out there and do what's necessary to win in a very controlled manner, with personality and with sportsmanship. Maintain your poise and character at all times."

This was it. The big dance. Pearl's chance to shake things up.

The Tigers wasted no time; even the way they approached pregame introductions was unlike anything the fans at Memorial Gym had ever seen. Rather than returning to the team bench or heading out to midcourt after the starting lineup had been introduced, the entire Tiger team—players and coaches alike—formed a tight circle, waists bent, hands clasped together down low in the middle of it all, the group linked as one, pulsing in and out, back and forth, up and down, like a beating heart about to explode. With the Tiger cheerleaders shrieking at the top of their lungs just a few feet away, Wallace's teammate Walter Fisher had to shout to be heard. He called out, and the guys, still pulsing, pulsing, pulsing, repeated: "Team!" *"Team!"* "Can't be beat!" *"Can't be beat!"* "Won't be beat!" *"Won't be beat!"* "All for one!" *"All for*

*one!" "*One for all!" *"One for all!"* "All for Pearl!" *"All for Pearl!"*
"Pearl High!" *"Pearl High!"*

To the modern eye, the black-and-white footage of the
1966 Tennessee high school championship game looks
positively ancient: the Chuck Taylor high-top sneakers, the
short shorts, the straight-up-and-down dribbling style,
the lack of contact between players, the unorthodox free
throw shooting. But every now and then, a flash of the
contemporary: Ted McClain's legs kicked up behind him on
a jumper, Perry Wallace skying for a rebound and making
an outlet pass to start a fast break. The next generation of
basketball was breaking through.

Pearl's McClain opened the game's scoring with his pat-
ented jumper, and throughout the early going, he and Walter
Fisher were as hot as ever from the outside. By the end of the
first quarter, Pearl led 16–10. By halftime, the Pearl lead had
grown to 31–18. There had been no dunks, only a couple of
fast breaks. The beauty of this effort was in how methodical
it was. All that remained now were two eight-minute quarters,
sixteen minutes to history.

But Treadwell forward Darrell Garrett began to heat up in
the third quarter, and guard Curry Todd's jumper was true.
When Todd took the fourth quarter's opening tip for Treadwell and scampered all the way down the court for a layup, the

lead was cut to five. The teams traded baskets for nearly five minutes, and when Wallace fouled Todd with 3:23 remaining, the Treadwell junior hit both free throws to cut Pearl's lead back down to five at 53–48. A McClain layup and another Todd jumper, and the lead was 55–50 with 2:39 left.

After the game, Wallace told *Tennessean* reporter Jimmy Davy it was at this moment he realized that if he wanted this victory bad enough, he could make it happen.

"I knew we had to have the ball," Wallace told Davy, "and I knew who could get it. Me."

When Todd misses a jumper, Wallace skies for the rebound, tosses a quick outlet pass downcourt to lead the break, and Fisher lays it in for two. The Pearl fans leap to their feet. Garrett misses, Wallace grabs another rebound, passes downcourt, and Fisher lays it in again. Tiger fans grow louder, a cascading crescendo reverberating off the cinder-block walls, the gym taking on the supercharged air that only comes when a team's supporters know a victory is at hand.

The Pearl players know it, too, and they finally begin to loosen up, Wallace leaping high again to grab another missed shot, his seventeenth rebound of the game, his legs kicked out to the side, his body forming a giant X as he snatches the ball in midair. His toss downcourt is straight over the top, like a baseball pitcher's, a rare flourish from the straight arrow. Next time down the court, McClain whips a behind-the-back pass to Douglas for an easy layup, and the romp is on and the game is over, the final score 63–54.

One moment in time, so many different reactions:

Over there, behind the bench, those are the Pearl cheerleaders, leaping high into the air and screaming with joy for their school.

Right on the court, there are Perry Wallace and all but one of his teammates, grabbing Coach Ridley and hoisting him to their shoulders, all smiles and hugs, holding their index fingers up in the air. Pearl's number one!

And there goes Walter Fisher, walking slowly past his celebrating teammates, exhausted from playing every minute of the game, head down, taking a seat on the Pearl bench, towel over his head, head in his hands. *Thank you, Jesus, we pulled this one off! Nobody got hurt; there were no mishaps. We made it through the entire season undefeated. We've got so much to be thankful for, Lord.*

And here comes Richard Baker, Memorial Gym custodian, a Vanderbilt employee since the 1940s, the only black man associated with the Commodore Athletic Department; here he comes with a ladder straight to the hoop next to the Pearl bench, just as he's done so many times before, setting up that ladder so the championship team can cut down the nets, only this time with an extra measure of pride.

After Governor Frank Clement presented the Tigers with the championship trophy, coach and players made their way back

Vanderbilt custodian Richard Baker hands Perry Wallace a net after the state championship game.

PHOTO BY JIMMY ELLIS, THE TENNESSEAN.

to their lockers in the bowels of the gym, where they were surrounded by reporters eager for quotes from the champs.

As usual, Ridley looked at the big picture.

"I'm especially happy for the other eighty Negro schools in the TSSAA who came in with us," he said. "We proved it could be done. A lot of folks thought we'd choke and get beat somewhere along the line, but these boys never faltered. I guess I was proudest of the fact that in all of our tournament games, regardless of what happened, our boys never seemed to lose their poise."

Showered and dressed, most of the Tigers had one thing on their mind: the postgame party. Eight people piled into the car teammate Tony Moorman's aunt had let him borrow, and the rest of the team followed close behind. Girlfriends showed up, and the whole crew partied late into the night and early the next morning. All but one guy.

Elated over the victory but still weary from a cold and fever that had dragged him down throughout the tournament, Perry Wallace rode home to Tenth Avenue with his parents, picked up a burger and milk shake along the way, and settled in for a late night of television. He fell asleep watching a horror movie, but before the flick had come on, he had watched a little basketball.

March 19, 1966, wasn't a date that would go down only in Tennessee high school basketball history.

That very same night, in College Park, Maryland, Texas

Western was taking on Adolph Rupp's Kentucky Wildcats for the NCAA men's basketball championship.

Perry Wallace drank his chocolate shake while watching the single most important college basketball game ever played.

Pearl players celebrate their state championship.

Chapter 10

The Promise

EVEN AS THE TIGERS WERE revolutionizing high school basketball in Tennessee, dozens of fans at Memorial Gym had
brought along portable televisions to watch the Kentucky–
Texas Western national championship game, which started just
as Pearl's victory was winding down.

Pearl student Lee Hayden walked home from the gym,
flipped on his black-and-white TV, and thought they must be
airing a replay of the Pearl-Treadwell game, what with five
black kids playing against five white kids. It took him a minute
before he realized he was watching Miners and Wildcats, not
Tigers and Eagles. All seven players Texas Western coach Don
Haskins put on the court were black; Adolph Rupp's Kentucky
Wildcats were all white.

While blacks across the country had a special rooting interest, Wallace had more personal reasons to stay glued to the set. David Lattin, Big Daddy D, the gym-rattling dunker who had been such a big influence on a young Wallace, was now Texas Western's biggest star. Wallace was struck by the similarities between the game he was watching and the game he had just played, right down to the fact that he had become Big Daddy D's Pearl High counterpart. Lattin commanded the attention of the Wildcats—and the nation—on Texas Western's second possession of the championship game. "Just dunk it like they ain't never seen it dunked," his coach instructed, and Big Daddy D obliged, slamming the ball off a Kentucky player's head on the way to a historic victory for the Miners.

Wallace had another reason to pay close attention: Kentucky was recruiting him. Though he was pulling for Texas Western, there were aspects of Kentucky's program that appealed to him. Most obvious was the winning tradition. In his lifetime, the Wildcats had won four national championships. Wallace also admired the Kentucky assistant coaches who were recruiting him: "They were just great," Wallace said. "I really liked them."

While Rupp was an unpopular figure among blacks because his teams were still all white, Wallace was only vaguely aware of that reputation. His opinion of the Wildcats was shaped more by the fact he had never met Rupp; his assistants had done all the recruiting. Given the enormity of the decision facing Wallace, the hardships he'd endure as a pioneer, he determined that he couldn't put his fate in the hands of a man who hadn't bothered to visit him.

"It wasn't that I wanted special treatment," Wallace explained, "it was that this was a special situation. Anybody that wouldn't lend that personal touch, I couldn't go there. To have the top guy say nary a word, that was a very important consideration."

Though many in Nashville felt it was only a matter of time until Wallace chose Vanderbilt—Vanderbilt wanted *him*, after all—that belief reflected a sense of certainty that simply didn't exist within Wallace's own mind. While Vanderbilt held an advantage, he enjoyed visiting other campuses, had a hard time dismissing the idea of heading north for college, and had reservations about remaining in Nashville for four more years.

By mid-April, Wallace still had not made a decision. Coach Skinner was working him hard, receiving indications that Wallace had Vandy high on his list. After Vanderbilt's student-run newspaper, the *Hustler*, ran an article on Wallace, a segment of Vanderbilt's student body was especially curious about Wallace's plans, wanting nothing more than to land the prize recruit. Then Nashville's morning newspaper, the *Tennessean*, devoted a two-page spread to the hometown prospect who was attracting so much national attention.

In every possible way, Wallace was portrayed as the all-American boy and the kind of guy anyone should want on their basketball team. Within a day or two, Coach Skinner was flooded with letters from Vanderbilt fans and alums.

They had seen Wallace play.

They had read about him in the paper.

And if Skinner signed Wallace to a scholarship, they wrote, they'd never attend another Vanderbilt basketball game again.

Skinner threw out the petitions demanding that he not recruit a black player as quickly as they arrived. The hateful letters represented only a minority of the Vanderbilt community, he believed. Plus, he knew Heard and the university were with him on this one, "and they were the ones who paid my check. I wanted to recruit Perry Wallace, and there wasn't anything those alums could do about it."

As the calendar turned from April to May, Perry began to feel mounting pressure to make a decision. "It's beginning to be clear what you want to do," his father told him. "You should go ahead and make your choice."

Teammates, friends, college recruiters, sportswriters—everyone had an opinion, but this was a decision Perry wanted to make on his own. Those other people weren't going to have to live with the consequences. Before he decided where to spend the next four years of his life, he knew exactly where he needed to spend the next hour: down in a clearing among the cliffs and trees over by White City Park.

For years, Perry had worked to strengthen his legs and his stamina by jogging around the neighborhood, winding his way up and down the steep hills. On one of these jogs, he discovered a hidden thicket of trees and rocks off to the side of Ninth Avenue. When he was stressed out by school, by racial tensions, by the everyday troubles of a teenager, this is where he came to sit and think in peace. Surrounded by nature in the heart of the city, he felt far from the troubling and hurried aspects of the world. But even beyond that, when he sat atop a rock in the clearing, he felt transported to a "mystical place," no longer confined to North Nashville, but ascended to one of the magical locations he was reading about in poetry class, "somewhere like Xanadu."

"And this," he said on a tour of his old neighborhood more than forty years later, looking at the very spot, "is where I went to do my last thinking about whether I would go to Vanderbilt."

Though he felt pressure from people whose opinions he respected, as he sat and meditated among the trees, Wallace was determined to make this critical decision on his own. There was a lot to like about Vanderbilt. He was impressed by the small campus and the engineering curriculum and was pleased to see that the basketball players took their schoolwork seriously. The team had a winning tradition and played in a major conference. Coach Skinner treated him and his parents with respect.

But more than anything, he was attracted by the promise. The promise that the world was changing, that the playing field was being leveled, that if you worked hard, played fair and made the right decisions, you could participate in the full measure of society whether you were white or black. With segregation dying, the America in which he'd live the rest of his life would require that he learn to interact with all different kinds of people. His teachers had prepared him for this moment, and he was ready to seize it.

Still, it was one thing to steel himself for the journey across town, another to ponder road trips to Alabama, Georgia, and Mississippi, going it alone deep in the heart of Dixie. He'd heard what a special opportunity it would be to become a pioneer in the Southeastern Conference, but what he was beginning to understand was how easy it was to talk about such a thing and how difficult it would be to actually live through it. As he climbed down from the rock and began to run back home, he knew that he had just made the decision to attend Vanderbilt University not because he would be a trailblazer, but in spite of it.

Chapter 11

The Surprise

ONE WEEK AFTER SIGNING HIS scholarship papers, Perry Wallace was shocked by a newspaper headline mentioning a second black player coming to Vanderbilt. Wallace had assumed he'd be alone on his journey as a pioneer. Now, just seven days after taking the first step to end the great migration of Southern black athletes to Northern campuses, Wallace was surprised to discover that he had already paved the way for a high-scoring black guard named Godfrey Dillard. Interestingly, Wallace had cleared Dillard's path to Vanderbilt not from another segregated public high school in the South but from an integrated Catholic school up North, in Detroit.

And while Wallace selected Vanderbilt only after reluctantly accepting the idea of becoming the SEC's first black ballplayer,

Wallace is joined by his parents, Perry Sr. and Hattie, as he appears with Vanderbilt coach Roy Skinner to officially announce his commitment to Vanderbilt.

PHOTO BY ELDRED REANEY, THE TENNESSEAN.

that notion was the only reason Dillard wanted to head south. Dillard wasn't particularly impressed by Coach Skinner, didn't put much stock in Vanderbilt's academic reputation. For Dillard, the opportunity to break a color line was irresistible, offering him the chance to contribute to the civil rights movement in a way that he felt wasn't possible in Michigan.

Dillard's decision to leave the North was especially striking given where he came from. Detroit had long attracted Southern blacks, its thriving factories making it a magnet for black laborers throughout the first half of the twentieth century. His parents had been a part of the migration, and for a brief time before his father died young of a heart attack, their experience had been a classic example of the opportunities the city afforded black families.

From the time he was seven years old, Godfrey was up at five o'clock each morning to begin his paper route, hurling newsprint into the front yards of the stately homes in the Boston-Edison neighborhood. As he traversed the wide, elm-shaded boulevards with his sack of papers, Godfrey saw accomplished blacks and whites living side by side in what was increasingly becoming "a very integrated, progressive neighborhood." Along with wealthy white businessmen, Boston-Edison was the home of many of Detroit's most successful blacks.

"In my neighborhood, I saw examples of black men who could succeed," Dillard recalled. "I saw a black lawyer who was successful. My next-door neighbor was a dentist; he was successful. There were a couple of black doctors who lived down the street. They had clean homes. They had nice cars. So as a young person, the idea that the Afro American could not succeed was not an issue to me."

Godfrey learned similar lessons about equality and opportunity each day at school. A smart, highly social kid with a quick smile, Godfrey became one of the most popular students at Visitation School. Godfrey was the school's best athlete, earning all-state honors in football and basketball and playing some baseball, too. While his mother wanted him to become a doctor or lawyer like the men along his paper route, Godfrey dreamed of becoming a professional athlete, which wasn't much of a surprise considering the sheer quantity of bats, balls, sticks, hoops, and pucks he'd been surrounded by his entire life. The Dillard home became one of the hubs of the neighborhood; all the kids, black and white, loved to come over and play.

Invited to take a look at Vanderbilt on a weekend recruiting visit during his senior year of high school in 1966, Dillard was eager to check out the campus and to see Nashville. His host on the trip was Commodore center Hal Bartch, a "big, muscular guy" from St. Louis. Bartch took his guest on a tour of the campus, and Dillard was impressed by the athletic facilities, especially Memorial Gymnasium and its wide, raised court. His mother and grandmother, both born and raised in the South, were strongly opposed to Godfrey's interest in Vanderbilt, wanting to protect him from a racism unlike anything he had experienced in Detroit.

But if his visit to Nashville was any indication of what it would be like to live there, Dillard believed, the women were being overprotective. Bartch took Godfrey out for steaks, and nobody gave the guys a second look. On campus, Dillard found himself surrounded by white students, but he was used to that. While his high school had a diverse student body, it was still mostly white. On his flight back to Detroit, Dillard had a good feeling about Vanderbilt.

"At first blush, it didn't appear to be that challenging of an environment," he said. "I didn't sense any discrimination on that visit."

On May 10, accompanied by a newspaper photographer, Coach Skinner visited Dillard and his family. Dillard's mother and grandmother were cordial to the coach but still squarely against the idea of Godfrey moving to the South. Black people were still getting lynched down there, they told him. Despite the protests of the women who had raised him, Dillard would not be swayed. He was overcome with excitement as he thought about signing the scholarship papers the coach had brought with him from Nashville, an act that would put him squarely in the forefront of the civil rights movement. He had considered himself a political figure at his high school, the first black student council president in his school's history, the leader of a small black community at a small school. He believed that signing those papers Skinner pushed across the table would allow him "to move the race forward." This is what the 1960s were all about, he told himself, breaking barriers in all facets of American life.

He signed the papers and smiled for the camera.

When it came to Godfrey Dillard and Vanderbilt University, he believed, "the sky was the limit."

Chapter 12

Dangerous Territory

"WE'RE NOT PREJUDICED," THE MEN told him, "but we think you'll understand why we have to do this."

It was a peaceful August Sunday morning, the men dressed conservatively in dark suits, speaking quietly but firmly, standing in a small room just inside the entrance to the University Church of Christ.

Perry Wallace had arrived on campus several weeks early to get a few math and science courses out of the way during the summer before his schedule became crowded with basketball practices in the fall. He wanted to get a feel for the campus, to slowly test the waters of integration. New faces, new sounds, new surroundings. And new twists on the familiar.

Perry had been a devout churchgoer each Sunday ever since

he had been baptized in the tiny pool at the Fifteenth Avenue Church of Christ. Attending a weekly sermon was as important a routine in his life as any. So in this summer of 1966, when Sundays came around, Perry had woken up early, put on a coat and tie, and walked over to the church Clyde Lee had recommended on one of Wallace's recruiting visits. The University Church of Christ was not affiliated with Vanderbilt but sat across the street from campus, a few blocks away from Wallace's dorm room.

Three or four Sundays, Wallace made the short walk to the chapel, quietly taking a seat in the back, the only black person in the place. A few folks would come by and say hello.

I know who you are.

I saw you play at Pearl.

Good luck at Vanderbilt.

Still, the room seemed cold to Wallace, as if the religion had been sucked out. He sat in the back pews and asked himself the same questions over and over: What are these people *doing* in here? Where was the spirituality?

Uncomfortable as he may have been, Wallace knew this was the first of many tests he would be confronted with as a pioneer. He'd give it a go.

Wallace made the short walk for the fourth or fifth Sunday in a row, prepared to sit quietly in the back, prepared, once again, to try to figure out how these congregants practiced their religion.

Then they stopped him at the door.

Perry, come with us.

He followed a group of church elders into a side room.

We're not prejudiced.

We think you'll understand.

Some people in the church don't like you being here.

They say they'll write the church out of their wills if you keep coming.

We can't have that.

You can't keep coming.

Do you understand?

You need to go.

Now.

"OK," Wallace said, "I understand."

He walked out the door, past the worshippers on their way in, and continued back to his dorm room, emotionless. The old survival mechanisms handed down through generations of segregation kicked in: at once, he later concluded, he was denying his feelings and accepting the cold reality of the situation.

"There was a dangerous automaticity about the responses to exclusion and segregation," he said. "You would try to suppress it or hide from it even as it was happening. Most of us at that point were not brave heroes, so we just said 'OK' in those situations. It was a lot easier to do that."

He entered his dorm room much earlier than planned,

loosened his tie, and sat down on his bed, coming to the realization that maybe America wasn't changing as quickly as he had been led to believe.

Wallace was reminded of the first time he had learned about segregation, as a five-year-old boy stepping onto a city bus with his mom. While his mother paid, he took a seat next to a white man, unaware this was forbidden for a black person, even a young boy, in Nashville at the time. Immediately, his mother rushed over and lifted Perry up, ushering him to the back of the bus. "While I still didn't understand what was going on, and it all seemed quite strange," Wallace recalled, "I did what Mama said. I played by the rules."

September 14, 1966. Cars from the Peach State, the Lone Star State, Sportsman's Paradise, the Land of Lincoln—and cabs from the Greyhound bus station—arrived on campus throughout the day, as 1,015 students began their studies at Vanderbilt. These freshmen were smart kids: Perry Wallace was one of fifty-five valedictorians, and about half of the new arrivals earned straight-A averages in high school.

Among these freshmen were some of the best and the brightest young black scholars in the country. It had been only two years since the university had begun allowing black students to attend, so it still felt like the "integration experiment" was just getting started.

From tiny Redfox, Kentucky, came Bobbie Jean Perdue, the first black valedictorian at integrated Carr Creek High School. A country girl in the big city, she was startled by the wealth of her new classmates.

"Here I was seeing girls come in with trailers attached to the family car with their belongings," Perdue recalled. "I arrived with a suitcase, and it was an old suitcase. And then I went to the bus station and got the wood trunk I had sent ahead."

Bedford Waters arrived from Knoxville, Tennessee, where as a child he drank from the "colored" water fountains and sat behind a white line that marked the back of the bus. His mother, a college graduate, worked for an insurance company, and his father was a pastry chef. From the time he was five years old, Bedford proclaimed that he wanted to grow up to be a doctor. "Go to college and better yourself," his parents stressed to their only child. When it was time to choose a college, Bedford's guidance counselor told him he should consider heading to Nashville. He earned a National Merit Scholarship and arrived at Vanderbilt with a can-do mind-set: "I'm going to do my best, get involved, not isolate myself, and compete with the best students because I'm good enough."

Carolyn Bradshaw came to Nashville from Winston-Salem, North Carolina. Growing up with two brothers and a single mom, Carolyn had always known that if she wanted to go to college, she'd have to earn a full scholarship. Attending segregated schools, she worked so hard that she was named valedictorian and earned a Rockefeller scholarship to Vanderbilt.

Morris Morgan, from Cedartown, Georgia, devised an ingenious plan to get to Vanderbilt. Because none of the historically black colleges in Georgia offered a chemical engineering major, and because Georgia Tech had yet to integrate, he declared his interest in chemical engineering and took advantage of Georgia's out-of-state aid program that essentially paid for blacks to study elsewhere. The child prodigy entered Vanderbilt at the age of *fifteen*.

For those few white students who bothered to pay attention, it was obvious that these pioneering students, while few in number, were no ordinary people.

Frye Gaillard was raised in what he considered a typical white Old South family. When he arrived at Vanderbilt as a freshman in the fall of 1964 along with the first black undergraduates, he was just beginning to question the assumptions of the Old South. Soon enough, his worldview was completely turned upside down.

"These brilliant young black people were so far ahead of me academically that the foolishness of that sort of Southern white assumption of superiority became immediately obvious," he recalled. "My black classmates were the living refutation of it. A black guy down the hall began to tutor me in calculus, because I was making an F and he was making an A. That's when it all clicked for me, understanding the society I had come from. It was like, 'Oh, we've really been a part of something bad.'"

Having returned home to Tenth Avenue for a few days when his summer program ended, Perry Wallace moved back to campus with the rest of the incoming freshmen on September 14. His father drove him and helped his son unpack a few suitcases and arrange his room at Vanderbilt Hall. Perry set out his favorite high school graduation present, a record player his sisters had bought for him. He lined up his records, a collection that included lots of jazz, some big band, some classical, and some Motown.

Godfrey Dillard arrived on campus later that same day, flying in from Detroit. He found his dorm room—also in Vanderbilt Hall—and began to unpack his clothes. Not five minutes later, there was a knock on the door.

It was Perry Wallace, there to welcome his new teammate. It was the first time they'd ever met.

They talked for an hour before there was another knock on the door. And another. And another. The few black students on campus were finding each other, and Dillard's room, one he hadn't even slept in yet, became the hub. The other students eventually drifted off to dinner or back to their own rooms, but Wallace remained. He and Dillard were getting along great, but they were also feeling each other out, discovering their similarities and differences.

They both felt that the other represented a certain stereotype. Dillard had traits of the "typical" Northern black of the day: he was louder, more assertive, more outwardly confident, carried himself with a swagger, acted as if he were in control of his own destiny. Wallace, the Southerner, was more reserved, more diplomatic, seemingly less confident, more aware of the hazards of the world they were entering.

Perry talked to Godfrey about growing up in Nashville, about his love for music, about the championships he had won at Pearl. He told Godfrey about the state of race relations in Nashville, some of the obstacles they were sure to encounter.

Godfrey talked to Perry about Detroit's own racial tensions, about the excitement of being a pioneer in the Southeastern Conference, the history they would make. As their conversation extended deep into the night, Godfrey got the sense that his new teammate appreciated his Northern sensibilities.

"I knew we were going to be very good friends right off the bat, and I knew I was much more outgoing than he was," Dillard said. "I sensed that I could influence him, because I had been a student leader in high school and could tell when someone was attracted to me and could pull them into my environment and we could work as a team. It was almost like we were very good complements. Perry had a sense of knowing the landscape that I didn't have."

Which, in Wallace's mind, was everything. He may have been intrigued by Dillard's bravado and impressed by his intellect, but that didn't mean he was ready to follow. For Dillard, the sky was the limit; Wallace, for all his naïveté, knew it wasn't that easy, not for a young black male in the South in 1966—particularly for a young black athlete. And especially for a young black athlete who was making history. A "regular" black student on campus would be somewhat invisible to the Vanderbilt community and the outside world—a black athlete, though, would find himself in the spotlight, totally exposed to controversy and criticism. There had been black students at Vanderbilt and elsewhere in the Southeastern Conference before, but Wallace and Dillard, the first black basketball players in the conference, were entering unchartered land.

In the wee hours of this, the very first night they met, Wallace sensed that Dillard was headed into dangerous territory.

Chapter 13

History Made Them Wrong

"So"—THE PROFESSOR SMIRKED—"they've let the niggers in after all."

Thus goes the story of how Walter Murray—Wallace's best friend, former Pearl High classmate, and now Vanderbilt classmate—was welcomed to English class on the first day of his freshman year.

The cold dose of reality Murray encountered as a Vanderbilt newcomer was not unique. For Eileen Carpenter, a fellow black student, the crash came gradually, and at first, Carpenter couldn't put her finger on what was happening. In the summer following her senior year of high school, a puzzling pattern repeated itself when she attended parties for incoming Vanderbilt freshmen.

She arrived at the receptions excited and happy, only to find herself standing alone with her plate of food while others in the room laughed and talked as if they all knew each other. "People were not mean or anything, and if they caught your eye, they'd smile, but I started having this sense that I was just kind of there, just being politely ignored," she recalled. "At the time, it did not occur to me that maybe it was because I was black."

Carpenter lived at home that freshman year, and her proud parents drove her to campus for her first English class. She walked into the classroom and sat next to another black girl. A white boy joined them in the second row, several seats to their right, and the rest of the class sat two or three rows behind, leaving a virtual buffer zone around the two black freshmen. "I remember thinking, 'This is really strange,'" Carpenter recalled. But again, it wasn't until later in the semester that she asked herself whether this was happening because she was black.

"For me, not having been exposed to in-your-face racism, I guess I didn't understand the very subtle forms of racism where you just don't exist, where you're just kind of ignored," she said. "I just knew I was very unhappy and something was wrong. Nobody called me nigger; nobody spat on me. In fact, it was just the opposite. Everyone was polite."

It wasn't until Carpenter sat alone in a campus dining room that everything began to click. A cat darted through the cafeteria, but nobody seemed to notice. "I remember thinking to myself, 'I'm just like that cat. I don't make any difference.' Nobody paid any attention. Nobody looked up. It was then that I started understanding what I was feeling and what was going on. You were not there. You didn't impact anyone's life. You could be totally ignored, and if you disappeared, nobody would notice."

These periods of isolation told only half the story. When not completely ignored, many black students, who numbered less than 1 percent of the student body, felt that they were on the receiving end of piercing stares from their white classmates.

Wallace accompanied a small group of white classmates to dinner one evening in the cafeteria at the women's quadrangle, a routine occurrence for the white students. But as Wallace waited in line to choose his food, he looked up and realized that every pair of female eyes in the room was focused right on him, the women's pinched faces betraying feelings of fear, hatred, or maybe both, he couldn't be sure. Wallace's mother had warned him to "stay away from the white girls," and now, before he could even take a bite to eat, it seemed to him that the smartest solution might be to just leave the room.

Accustomed to being a big man on campus in high school, Dillard was disturbed by the eerie silence as he walked to his classes at Vanderbilt, nobody saying a word to him. Back in his dorm, the opposite extreme: cries of "nigger on the floor" accompanied by slammed doors.

On weekends, with few social options available, many black students spent lonely nights in their dorm rooms, listening to the loud and wild fraternity parties outside. Dillard was struck by the fact that frats would not accept black members but would frequently hire black bands to perform at their parties. Just walking past a frat house late on a Friday or Saturday night could be a distressing experience, former student Bedford Waters recalled. "They'd holler things as you were walking back to your dorm," he said. "'Nigger, what are you doing here? Go home, go back, you're not wanted here!'"

Wallace said he and his black classmates did the best they could to make the most of their days at Vanderbilt. For some, this meant attempting to do the same things white students took for granted. Unaware that none of the Vanderbilt sororities admitted blacks, Eileen Carpenter arrived on campus thinking she was going to "have a great time and join a sorority like the college days you saw on TV." She walked past all the sorority houses and picked the one she liked best—Kappa Alpha Theta. Carpenter attended the sorority's first rush party, and everything seemed to be going just fine. But when Carpenter's aunt came to visit one day, Eileen told her all about her plans.

"She looked at me like my head had just dropped off my body," Carpenter recalled. "She said, 'You can't join a sorority there; they won't allow Negroes.'"

Still, because most of the frat parties during the fall semester were ostensibly open to all students, not just frat members and their dates, Carpenter found the courage to walk in and try to have some fun from time to time. By her junior year, she noticed that as the night grew later, nobody seemed to care what color she was.

Carolyn Bradshaw noticed the same thing, more than once dancing the night away underneath a Confederate flag in the KA house. "It wasn't like you walked around the campus in fear," she recalled.

As many painful racial slights as she endured, Bobbie Jean Perdue said there was also always a group of white students who were helpful, who made sure she wouldn't have to eat alone.

Perry Wallace remembers those early days at Vanderbilt, when black and white students were trying to figure each other out—succeeding and failing, improvising, accepting and rejecting.

"People talked about, 'Let's all come together, and we'll all get along.' Nope, we had too much practice *not* getting along," Wallace says. "A lot of us blacks had to practice not feeling inferior after all of that segregation bull. There were a lot of whites who had to practice not feeling superior. We had a chance to practice at Vanderbilt, and some of us did. Some blacks and whites practiced and got better and better. The people who decided that 'Oh, blacks don't have anything to offer, and I don't need to be around them, and in fact I can do better not being around them, and the world is my father's world and my grandfather's world,' they may have been right *then*. But history made them wrong, progress made them wrong."

Segregation doesn't need any extra condemnation, Wallace says. Its evils speak for themselves. There's a certain level of decency everyone should be afforded. But look at who was so often ignored at Vanderbilt in 1966: the best and brightest black students from North and South, the class presidents, the valedictorians, the salutatorians.

"Just think about the stories we had to tell," Wallace said. "The students on campus who rejected us, who ignored us, who isolated us—we brought the opportunity for them to 'practice being equal.' The irony is that we were just who they needed to know. We brought with us insights into the world that they lived in that they did not have because segregation had set people apart. We had the other half of the story about race. And we were articulate messengers."

Yet not everyone cared to hear, much less listen.

Chapter 14

Hit or Miss

THE SQUEAKS OF THE SNEAKERS and the thud of the bouncing ball were always amplified in Vanderbilt's Memorial Gym, caroming off the cinder-block walls in the cavernous building. Those sounds were familiar to the "railbirds," a group of Commodore basketball fans who slipped out of work to watch practice every day. But there was a new, unfamiliar sound in November 1966: it was the voice of the freshman guard from Detroit, confident Godfrey Dillard, full of energy and yammering to anybody who'd listen as he high-dribbled the ball down the court. *Come out and get me! Come out and get me! Ahhh, get back, you need to move away, I'm taking it to the basket!*

Wallace and Dillard were a contrast in styles. While Godfrey yammered nonstop, Perry barely said a word, the kind of player who showed up early for practice, nodded his head when asked to do something, and then stayed late to work on an aspect of his game—alone. In some ways, Wallace was exhibiting the same work ethic and respect for authority that had always been fundamental to his personality: he did what the coaches asked, didn't pick fights with his teammates or opponents, didn't talk trash.

This is who he was in any setting, a personality shaped by, and consciously developed to manage, the realities of segregation. He believed that everything he said or did on the court reflected not only on him, but also on an entire race. In his behavior, he believed, he could either confirm or refute stereotypes and earn respect for himself and for blacks through hard work and strong character. All told, it was a traditional, conservative approach to integration that reflected Wallace's experiences growing up in the South. He could see that while Dillard was expressing himself in an entirely different way, they were both trying to make the same point: "I belong." While Wallace made his case gradually, largely keeping quiet, Dillard shouted it loud and clear.

Many of the other freshman players came from integrated Midwestern high schools, and had played with or against blacks before. No Vanderbilt players protested Wallace's recruitment; nobody transferred or threatened to quit. Benign neglect was the most serious offense for most of the guys: we'll

Wallace fights for a rebound in the 1966 freshman-varsity game, his first action as a collegiate player.

PHOTO BY BILL PRESTON, THE TENNESSEAN.

go our way, Perry will go his. Many chose to leave Wallace alone—no special treatment, the way he'd want it, they told themselves—at a time when he needed them most.

"I remember vaguely having the feeling that Perry was introverted, just like I was," recalled student manager Gene Smitherman. "He was not the kind of person who needed to go out and be your best buddy. This is what bothers me, forty years later, is that it was almost like, 'Let Perry be.' I'm wondering if Perry needed more than he got from me and from others as well."

The chartered bus rolled north along US Highway 31, bound from Nashville to Bowling Green, carrying the Commodores' traveling contingent to the campus of Western Kentucky University for the 1966–67 season opener. Seated up front were the coaches; chattering away in the next few rows were the student managers, the team trainer, and the sportswriters. Players from the varsity and the freshman teams settled into the remaining seats for the sixty-five-mile trip across the border into Kentucky.

The game would literally be the biggest thing that had ever happened on campus at WKU, defending champions of the Ohio Valley Conference. A crowd of more than thirteen thousand packed into Diddle Arena, the largest gathering of people for any campus event in the school's history. With four returning starters, Western was expected to achieve even greater things than the 1966 team, which had placed third in the NCAA Mideast regionals.

By 5:30 p.m., it was time for the Commodore freshmen to take the court. As the ball was tipped into action, Wallace and Dillard became the first blacks to play for an SEC team in an official game, freshman or varsity.

Diddle Arena was an ideal spot for Wallace and Dillard to begin their careers. With black stars such as Clem Haskins suiting up for the Western varsity team that night, the crowd was accustomed to the sight of black players, and with such high expectations for the Hilltoppers, all the focus was on the home team. Two blacks on the opponents' freshman squad were of little consequence.

But to the Vanderbilt fans who made the trip, and to the Commodore varsity players who watched the freshman game from the bleachers, the game was transformational: the new look of SEC basketball unfolded before their eyes.

Dillard pushed the ball quickly up the court, alternately feeding the ball to teammates for open jumpers or taking the ball to the rim himself. Wallace owned the paint, leaping high for rebounds and running the floor for dunks. On one possession, an errant Commodore shot bounced high off the rim, and Vanderbilt fan Bob Calton was dumbfounded to see Wallace shoot straight up in the air like a rocket, catch the ball, and slam it through the basket in one motion.

Godfrey Dillard's Detroit style took some Commodore teammates by surprise.
Dillard wore Jackie Robinson's number, 42.

"Obviously nobody at Vanderbilt had ever been able to do that before," Calton recalled.

In the end, Dillard scored sixteen points and Wallace capped off an eighteen-point, twenty-one-rebound effort with a left-handed slam dunk in the final minutes that sealed a 73–65 win for Vanderbilt.

Following on the heels of a successful first game for Wallace and Dillard, bad news came the very next day: the University of Mississippi canceled both of its upcoming freshman games against Vanderbilt. The decision was startling—why would Ole Miss cancel the games on such short notice?

In fact, the reason was obvious: what better way to limit opportunities for black players in the SEC than to deny their very existence?

Ole Miss coach Eddie Crawford didn't say that outright, of course. He made excuses, announcing he had suddenly discovered that he had double-booked his squad on January 14, and instead of hosting Vanderbilt, the Rebel freshmen would instead be taking on John C. Calhoun State Junior College. As for the February 11 game, Crawford told *Sports Illustrated*, the Rebels would not make the 240-mile trip to Nashville "on account of school work." The magazine noted that in place of the supposedly too-taxing trip to Vandy, the Rebels would instead make a 175-mile trip to Newton, Mississippi, to play

Clarke Memorial College. Crawford and Ole Miss athletic director Tad Smith denied that the presence of Wallace and Dillard had anything to do with the announcement.

"You newspaper people are always trying to make something out of nothing," the coach told a caller from the Vanderbilt *Hustler*.

If it was all a coincidence, that was nearly impossible to believe anywhere outside Mississippi. "Everybody," Wallace said, "knew that wasn't true."

Despite the discouraging news out of Oxford, the vibe around the Commodore program was overwhelmingly positive. Vanderbilt's home opener against Southern Methodist University on December 3 was attended by a sellout crowd of 9,222. Commodore basketball tickets remained the hottest thing in town, and with Wallace on the way up to the varsity team in a year, demand for tickets was expected to intensify.

Prior to the varsity's game against SMU, the freshman team played Pensacola Junior College, and Wallace dominated, scoring twenty-three points while grabbing twenty-four rebounds. Wallace's playing career would soon come to be marked by near constant stress, but for now he was having fun.

When Middle Tennessee State University came to Memorial, it provided a chance for Wallace to square off against one of his old high school rivals. MTSU's Ken Riley was a six-foot-six leaper whom Wallace described as a "savage dunker." The freshman game took on the air of one of those rollicking dunkathons at Pearl High, with Wallace and Riley exchanging thunderous jams to the delight of the crowd. By game's end, Wallace had produced six dunks and nineteen rebounds, but Vanderbilt lost the game 68–64 in overtime.

In that game, Wallace suffered a groin injury that limited his mobility, leaping ability, and productivity for the entire second half of the season. He played through the pain, a suffering that was intensified, he said, because nobody seemed too concerned about his well-being, especially a few vocal fans who sat close to the court. He could hear them hollering. *You're just like a horse, you get out there and play! You play until we're finished with you!*

"I felt really abused by that," Wallace recalled. "I wanted more treatment for the pain, not to be treated like an animal."

All of a sudden, the season—and Wallace's day-to-day life—took a downhill turn. The freshman team started losing, and Wallace's groin continued to hurt throughout the season. To make matters worse, his mother increasingly showed signs of a serious illness, and feelings of isolation on campus intensified. Wallace grew painfully lonely and unhappy. He spent long nights alone in his dormitory, thinking about what lay ahead of him in the classroom and on the basketball court, praying to God for the support he wasn't finding anywhere else.

He found a brief reprieve in Lexington, Kentucky, home of Adolph Rupp's Wildcats, the team that to some had symbolized the old, white, traditional brand of basketball in the previous season's title game against Texas Western. Still, Rupp routinely scheduled games against teams with black players, home and away, when many other SEC teams would not. UK fans, Wallace concluded over his four years at Vanderbilt, cared only about winning games and watching good basketball. In an atmosphere like this, he could relax, play his game, not be subjected to a barrage of epithets he anticipated receiving on the road in Mississippi and other parts of the Deep South. Best of all, he could test his skills against elite competition. Playing against Kentucky, he believed, was as close as it came in the SEC to what he imagined it would have been like if he had gone to a school in the North: basketball for basketball's sake, no extra baggage.

Almost.

After more than five decades, the particulars of individual plays within specific games have faded from the memories of the men associated with the 1966–67 Vanderbilt freshman basketball team, but many of them vividly remember this: Perry Wallace leaping high in the air for an offensive rebound, grabbing the ball, and slamming it through the basket over the defenseless arms of Kentucky star and future NBA Hall of Fame forward Dan Issel.

It was a dramatic scene in its own right, but what came next is what everyone remembers most: an old man watching the dunk and going ballistic, complaining about the affront to fundamental basketball.

It was Adolph Rupp.

"It was just a flash; I saw him as I was running back down the floor," Wallace recalled. "He was upset, and I saw him over on the side complaining about the dunking." Years later, Wallace suspected that it wasn't this one dunk alone that caused Rupp to throw a fit; it was the context of it. Wallace had just given Rupp an ugly flashback to his championship loss to Texas Western the previous year. Big Daddy Lattin's dunk had set the tone for UK's loss in the NCAA title game. "And now, I was right there in the conference," Wallace said, "ready to dunk on his team. It must have been an exclamation point on a terrible sentence in Rupp's mind."

To Rupp, the dunk was likely the ultimate symbol of the new, flashier, and, in his opinion, inferior and less pure style of basketball. It was also a move, at the time, that was associated with African Americans such as NBA greats Wilt Chamberlain and Bill Russell, and college stars David Lattin and Lew Alcindor.

Despite that dunk, UK still blew out Vanderbilt, 85–64. Nevertheless, Wallace played well, scoring fourteen points, grabbing twenty-one rebounds, and blocking several shots. After the loss, Wallace took a seat in the stands to watch the

Though Wallace has long remembered angering legendary Kentucky coach Adolph Rupp with a slam dunk during a freshman game in the 1966–67 season, he also recalled his games against UK as the most enjoyable of his SEC career.

VANDERBILT UNIVERSITY ATHLETIC DEPARTMENT.

varsity, where he was approached by Louisville *Courier-Journal* sportswriter Billy Reed.

"Life isn't one big holiday right now," Wallace told Reed. "I know it's going to be rough, and I wonder if I'll make it, but that's when I get support from God."

With Rupp's angry display fresh on his mind and an ominous road trip to Starkville, Mississippi, on the horizon, a sense of foreboding was growing in Wallace's gut. He was preparing himself for the crises he knew lay ahead.

"I've got to adapt and look at things not as pressures but as challenges," the eighteen-year-old confessed. "Life has been a series of challenges for me. I've just tried to meet them as they come along. If I come through now, I'll be a better man for it. It's a hit or miss thing. Either I'll make it or I won't."

Chapter 15

Crazy People

WHILE OLE MISS HAD CANCELED its games against the Commodores, Mississippi State did not.

Was that necessarily a good thing?

None of the Vanderbilt freshman team's previous road games had taken place any farther south than Nashville, so this was Godfrey Dillard's first foray into the dangerous Deep South his mother and grandmother had worried about. In Knoxville, orange-clad fans had shouted racist insults at Wallace and Dillard during the game against Tennessee, but Dillard knew this trip to Mississippi was different even before their plane rolled to a stop on the tarmac.

Less than three years had passed since Chaney, Goodman, and Schwerner, three civil rights activists, had been murdered only about sixty miles from Starkville, and less than a year had passed since another civil rights trailblazer, James Meredith, the first black student to attend the University of Mississippi, had been shot in broad daylight, even while surrounded by FBI agents, in nearby Hernando.

As Perry Wallace stepped on the court at Mississippi State, on the day he would later describe as his own version of hell on earth (remember Chapter 1?), racist fans "were screaming and hollering and insulting us, calling us names, saying they were going to kill us."

The threat was real, and Perry Wallace could feel it deep in his bones.

"You had a whole gym full of people just raining down on you," he remembers. "Here they were, all these Mississippi bigots, so loud and so close, and it was harsh. It was just awful, and it was the first time I'd ever dealt with this kind of stuff."

Most distressing of all, Wallace and Dillard were dealing with this madness all by themselves. No fair-minded Mississippi State fan called on the hecklers to stop. No ushers escorted unruly fans out of the arena. And certainly no Mississippi policeman was going to come to the defense of the black visitors from Nashville.

Before Jackie Robinson broke Major League Baseball's color line, Brooklyn Dodgers general manager Branch Rickey sat Robinson down to talk about the heckling and threats he was about to encounter. Robinson's managers repeatedly stood firm against white players on the Dodgers' and opponents' rosters who protested Robinson's presence. Black fans by the tens of thousands showed up in Chicago and Cincinnati and other National League outposts to support Robinson during his rookie season of 1947.

But here in the fire of Starkville, Wallace and Dillard received no such show of support: they scanned the crowd and found no black faces. And not here in Mississippi nor back in Nashville nor anywhere else did Coach Skinner or freshman team coach Homer Garr ever sit the Commodores down and talk about the unique nature of their teammates' situation, the need to show support on the road, to do their parts to defuse tense situations, to have their teammates' backs.

So none of his teammates said or did anything as Dillard's uniform grew cold and wet as the first half wore on, soaked with his own sweat, but also from spit flying out of the stands and from Cokes dumped on him when he ventured close to the sideline. No one came to his defense.

"These people are crazy," Dillard whispered to Wallace.

As the game wore on, the clock ticked down under five seconds before halftime, Vanderbilt trailing 43–39. Wallace found himself with the ball sixty feet from the basket, and he threw it downcourt in desperation. Team manager Paul Wilson watched Wallace launch the errant heave, simultaneously hearing a shriek from the crowd he'd remember four decades later: *Shoooot, niggggggerrrrrrr!*

Mack Finley, a white graduate student at Mississippi State who had grown up in West Tennessee, was shocked by the disgusting words and threats directed at Wallace, who bravely kept his focus on the game, pretending he didn't hear the slurs of the bigots.

"It was the ugliest thing I have ever seen in my life, the way they treated that man," Finley recalled. "I was ashamed to be from [the South]. I have seen a lot of ugly things, but nothing like that."

At halftime, the Commodores filed back into the decrepit locker room, which now, given what he'd just experienced out on the court, felt to Wallace like the dungeon of a medieval castle.

"Bear in mind the dramatic effect of that," Wallace said. "This dirty, rinky-dink place just accentuated how horrible the situation was. You're in this dump, and you have all this hell breaking loose. We knew we were going to have to go out into this madness for another half, and you don't know if anything worse is a possibility."

As Coach Garr delivered his halftime pep talk, the white players listened intently to his instructions, oblivious to—or maybe just ignoring—the torment Wallace and Dillard were experiencing. Expected to be listening to their coach, the black freshmen turned their focus inward instead.

"We were trying to be in denial," Wallace said. "We didn't want it to be this bad. But it was such an outrageous display of racism, like the blaring of trombones. The crowd was starting to shatter our denial."

The fact that none of their coaches or teammates acknowledged the hatred directed at them made a grotesque scene all the more bizarre, Wallace recalled. "Nobody was saying anything about it, and that was always part of the insanity."

Seated next to each other in the dungeon of a house of horrors as Coach Garr continued to deliver his halftime instructions, looking for support and finding none, the powerful forward from Nashville and the cocky guard from Detroit, determined not to sink, found strength in each other. Quietly, secretly, the teenagers clasped hands and held tight. No words were spoken, but the message was clear: *We're going to survive this.*

The survival instinct played out in entirely different, but characteristic, ways in the second half.

Wallace remained cautious. "You needed to make sure that there wasn't some kind of incident," he said. "You bump into another player or there's a collision, and the crowd gets fired up and they decide to do something during the game or after the game. If people are threatening to kill you, saying they're going to lynch you, then you don't know whether these are just empty threats or not."

Dillard's approach could not have been more different. A

foul is called, the action stops, Dillard lines up to shoot a free throw, all eyes on him, all the taunts directed at him, *nigger* this, *coon* that, and what does he do? He stops, smiles, and waves to the crowd. The catcalls continued to rain down loudly from the bleachers.

Though he didn't confront his friend, Perry was not pleased with Dillard's antics. "I was thinking, 'Godfrey, please don't do that!'" Wallace recalled. "It worked out OK, but this was a world that I had a better sense of than he did, and my approach was that you acted like nothing was going on. Don't give them anything that can escalate the situation to another level."

Later, dribbling the ball down the court, Dillard taunted his defender all the way. *Uh-oh, here I come!* "You *know* I was talking trash during the Mississippi State game," he said. "It became an us-against-them kind of thing. We were in the lion's den, but I was too young or too stupid or whatever to realize how dangerous the situation was. I decided that this was why we came to Vanderbilt."

Wallace and Dillard may have handled the pressure in entirely different ways, but each got results: Wallace led both teams with nineteen rebounds. Dillard was Vanderbilt's second-leading scorer, with sixteen points. Though Mississippi State won the game, 84–70, if ever two basketball players deserved a "mission accomplished, now let's get out of here" moment, this was it.

But with the varsity game still to come, not only would Wallace and Dillard have to stick around for that game to end before they could fly home, they'd have to jump from the frying pan into the fire by having to watch the varsity game from the bleachers behind the Vanderbilt bench, right in the middle of the crowd. Dillard was pelted with wads of paper, but curiously enough, the crowd quickly grew tired of harassing him and Wallace.

"Once we left the floor and took a seat in the stands, everything converted to an ordinary college basketball game, because you had white players playing against white players," Wallace said. "Godfrey and I were just sitting in the stands, and I guess they were finished with us anyway. They didn't choose to continue the taunting. That was it."

As Vanderbilt's plane soared back through the cold February sky from Starkville to Nashville, Wallace gazed out at the stars, thinking back to nine months earlier, when he had accepted a scholarship to Vanderbilt aware that there would be difficulties but still full of hope. That hope had been dashed in many ways and places—in the lobby of the University Church of Christ, in his own lonely room—and now here in Starkville, Mississippi, came the most painful proof, he believed, that his hope had been misplaced. What could he really expect from America?

Most painful of all, he thought about his mother, had been thinking about her all day. Wallace hadn't told any of his teammates the news, but just before the game, he had learned that she was on her way to Vanderbilt Hospital for an emergency surgery to treat the colon cancer that would eventually take her life. Not only had he feared for his own life that day in Starkville, he had feared for that of his mother. Lying in pain in her hospital bed, Mrs. Wallace listened to her son's game on the radio.

She could hear the crowd.

Chapter 16

Sudden Impact

As DIFFICULT AS THE ROAD games were for Perry Wallace, life wasn't always that much easier back on campus in Nashville. At a time when Wallace, Dillard, and the other black students at Vanderbilt were searching for opportunities to express themselves on a Southern, white campus, dealing with injustices big and small, discovering that promises of equal treatment were often hollow, and taking the first steps to organize themselves in a meaningful way, they looked outward for cues on how to proceed. In 1967, the civil rights leaders Martin Luther King Jr. and Stokely Carmichael embodied the two most likely paths.

King's path to racial justice was one focused on nonviolent protest and the promise of integration. Twenty-five-year-old

Stokely Carmichael, on the other hand, was the country's most outspoken advocate for the more aggressive, separatist Black Power movement.

The fact that those two famous and controversial men were about to set foot on the sedate Vanderbilt campus to speak at the university's highly regarded, student-run "Impact" speaker series was as mind-boggling as it was welcome.

"It was really daring and innovative and radical," former student Eileen Carpenter recalled, "and that was amazing for Vanderbilt at that time."

On April 7, 1967, Wallace, Dillard, Carmichael, and thousands of others entered Memorial Gym for Impact's opening session, featuring remarks by Dr. King. Preparing for the worst, in case racial tensions escalated, members of the Metro Police Department's intelligence division had already searched the gym on two separate occasions, and eighty-five officers, including forty in plain clothes, were scattered throughout the lobby and the bleachers. Six traffic officers were stationed outside the gym, and patrol cars circled the perimeter, ready for any disturbances.

Dressed in his familiar dark suit and tie, King defended his belief in nonviolence while acknowledging the forces that led to violent outbursts in urban areas. "I will continue to condemn riots because they cause more social problems than they solve," he said. "But we must condemn the conditions which make people feel compelled to riot. As long as justice for all people is postponed, there will continue to be riots. . . . The summers of riots are caused by the winters of delay."

Listening to Dr. King speak was a memorable experience for many of the students, including Wallace's friend Bedford Waters.

"You just walked out of there so mesmerized and inspired that there was hope," Waters recalled. "It was the first time I had seen him, and it was an overwhelming experience."

But as Waters returned to his dormitory energized by King's remarks, a time bomb was already ticking. The worst race riot in Nashville history was about to explode.

Just a few hours before his speech was set to begin at Vanderbilt on April 8, Stokely Carmichael found himself in the unlikeliest of environments—sitting down for lunch at Vanderbilt's Kappa Sig fraternity house with scores of (nearly all white) Vandy students. Wallace attended the lunch as well, and though he believed that his role as a trailblazer left him in no position to assume a radical stance, he was intrigued by the forceful tone struck by Carmichael.

For Wallace, part of the emotional experience that afternoon was to live vicariously through the responses Carmichael issued to Wallace's white classmates. One finely dressed young man of the South told Carmichael that whites would be more accepting of reasonable, "articulate" blacks than they would of Black Power types.

"No, you're still not going to let them in," Carmichael replied. "You're still going to treat them like a bunch of niggers." The student grew visibly angry. "That's all right, you can get mad and upset," Carmichael continued, "just don't burn down my churches."

Wallace was stunned to see this exchange taking place on his campus. "It was really striking to have these Vanderbilt students, whom we knew well, have to confront the idea of an outrageous black man who talked about race forcefully and did not back off."

Any time traveler looking for the most condensed snapshot of the opposing worldviews shaping America in the 1960s would be hard-pressed to pick a better time and place than the hours between 11:00 a.m. and 4:00 p.m. Central Time on Saturday, April 8, 1967, in Nashville, Tennessee. Before the fraternity house luncheons, Senator Strom Thurmond, a segregationist from South Carolina who had a long history of fighting against equal rights for black people, had laid out his conservative case; Carmichael would speak at 3:00.

In an address interrupted alternately by applause and snickering, Thurmond called for law and order and condemned King's tactics of civil disobedience. Arguing that civil rights protestors had no right to break the law, Thurmond quoted the Bible: "Slaves, obey your earthly masters, with fear and trembling, single-mindedly, as serving Christ." This drew laughter from the crowd as, a day earlier, King had predicted Thurmond would quote this very passage from the Bible.

With that, Thurmond was gone less than six hours after he had arrived, telling Vanderbilt students that he refused to share a platform with King or Carmichael.

And then, there he was, the man who had inspired death threats and the ire of so many white Americans. There was Stokely Carmichael in the flesh, walking to the podium, cheers bouncing off cinder blocks, his shadow dancing against the red, white, and blue backdrop.

Someone in the upper balcony unfurled a Confederate flag. Police quickly snatched up the flag and confiscated it, and then Carmichael repeated the line he had used at lunch. "That's OK, you can express your views, just don't burn down my churches." Carmichael began reading his prepared remarks, speaking about the causes and goals of the Black Power movement.

"The racial and cultural personality of the black community must be preserved. The community must win its liberation while preserving its cultural identity. This is the essential difference between integration as it is currently practiced and the concept of Black Power."

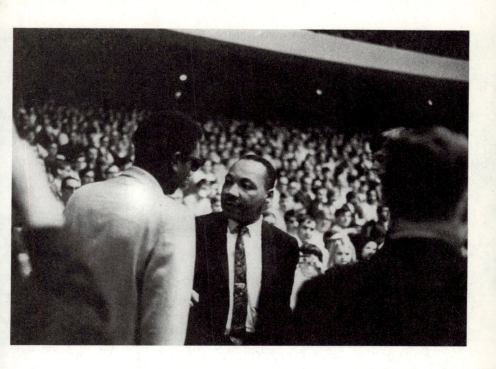

Civil rights leaders Stokely Carmichael and Martin Luther King Jr. exchange greetings at Vanderbilt's Impact Symposium in 1967.

Impact '67 was over, a rousing success. Despite concerns over bomb threats, demonstrations, and general unruliness, the Vanderbilt event had gone smoothly.

The events that soon followed in other parts of town, however, would not.

Problems started around 8:00 p.m., when the black owner of a restaurant near the historically black Fisk University called police to remove a disorderly student from the premises. Within minutes, word spread about the incident, and a group of black students, perhaps primed for action against authority after Carmichael's poking and prodding all week, began picketing outside the restaurant. Tensions grew more heated when Nashville police arrived on the scene around 9:00 p.m., a force that eventually exceeded four hundred officers, many of whom were itching for a confrontation in this part of town after being repeatedly warned about the potential for Carmichael to cause trouble.

One of the first to arrive at the scene of the confrontation was local newspaper photographer Dale Ernsberger, who was white. No sooner had he arrived to meet *Tennessean* reporter Frank Sutherland than the back windshield of his car was smashed to pieces by a rock thrown by rioters. Another rock bounced off the car and hit Sutherland in the head, the first of nine blows the reporter would take from rocks, bottles, and bricks that night.

Later, when a cabdriver hired to run film back to the newspaper from the scene was asked to return to the area of violence, his reply was predictable: "You haven't got enough money to pay me to go back there."

Meanwhile, Walter Murray's girlfriend and Wallace's friend, Donna, was studying in her dorm room at Fisk University when some classmates entered to tell her that Stokely Carmichael himself was down at the restaurant and that a big crowd was building outside. She put down her biology book and headed out to see what all the commotion was about. Carmichael was nowhere to be seen ("He was probably long gone if he had ever even been there at all," she recalled), but Donna noticed a man, too old to be a student, walking back and forth through the crowd, picking up rocks. Just as she said to herself, "What's he doing?" the guy began throwing the rocks at the police. Donna was stunned and found herself glued to the spot, trying to figure out what was going on.

"Cease and desist!" came the call from the police.

But more rocks came flying, the cops started firing their guns into the air, and *bam!*, someone threw Donna to the ground to protect her, her glasses tumbling out of sight. *I'm going to be blind in the middle of a riot!* she thought, but then she found her glasses and took off running for the safety of her dorm, passing by a group of students who were pushing a car back and forth in an attempt to flip it over.

Back in her dormitory, Donna saw girls throwing glass bottles out their windows to their boyfriends below, encouraging them to join the fray. "It was one scary night," she said.

As the riots continued, students—nearly eight hundred strong, according to some estimates— shouted "Black Power," threw rocks and bottles, and fired pellet guns off the metal helmets of police officers. Police retaliated by firing shots into the air and, in at least one case, aiming a tear gas canister into a Fisk dormitory. FBI agents arrived on the scene and called for reinforcements soon after midnight.

Just like Donna, Perry Wallace had been in the area, too, having followed Carmichael's entourage back to Fisk following the Vanderbilt speech because he'd heard that Stokely would be making one more address to students there. As Carmichael's rhetoric grew more heated than it had been at Vanderbilt, even

More than four hundred Nashville police officers took to Jefferson Street and other parts of North Nashville on the night of the 1967 Nashville riots.

Nashville Banner Archives, Nashville Public Library, Special Collections.

before the incident at the restaurant, Wallace began to suspect he was in the wrong place at the wrong time. He decided to walk back to the Vanderbilt campus.

"Stokely was talking, and the students were getting fired up," Wallace recalled. "A lot of times, you can feel the thing brewing, and you can tell something is going to blow. For me there were extra dangers in getting caught up in something like that, so I just took off."

Back at her parents' house in North Nashville, Wallace's classmate Eileen Carpenter had been unaware of what was happening down the street. She had the house to herself and had invited Carmichael and some of her fellow black classmates, including Godfrey Dillard, over to share ideas on how they could start an Afro American student association. Carpenter figured Carmichael would have ideas on how to organize the group.

Her guests waited for Carmichael, milling around the kitchen, dining room, and living room of the Carpenters' split-level house, until Eileen's friend Cynthia McClennon came through the door, and by the look on her face, Carpenter knew something was wrong.

"They're rioting at Fisk, and it's really wild!" McClennon announced to the group.

Carpenter turned on the radio and heard reports of the uprising, including rumors that Carmichael had started it all. She turned down the volume. "Well, because of all this," she said dejectedly, "I guess Stokely is not coming."

Then, another knock on the door. In walked Stokely Carmichael.

"I will always remember that," Dillard recalled. "We're listening to the radio about how Stokely Carmichael is out leading a riot, and the guy is standing right across from me."

By the time Carmichael departed and the Vanderbilt students drove back across town to their dorms, the situation on campus was beyond tense. Vanderbilt administrator K. C. Potter drove around town with campus police until 4:00 a.m., patrolling the area near the riots to see if the violence would spill over toward the campus and to gather intelligence in case a march against Vanderbilt was planned.

Nothing of the sort ever happened, although Potter returned to campus when several bomb threats against one of the school's dormitories were called in to the campus security desk. The decision was made to evacuate the building, and bleary-eyed students began to congregate in front of the fourteen-story red-brick dormitory that had opened in March. Its name? Carmichael Towers. Seems that the would-be bombers were unaware that the building was named for former chancellor Oliver Carmichael, believing instead that the school had so quickly fallen head over heels in love with its Impact speaker that it had already named a building for Stokely Carmichael.

All in all, skirmishes between police and roving bands of students lasted well into the early morning (and continued again the following night). Remarkably, in the end, there were relatively few injuries or arrests considering the scope of the unrest—around a dozen injuries and forty arrests.

Still, the riots were the first major social disorder in the nation in 1967, and the worst ever in Nashville.

The environment Wallace and Dillard would have to operate in had reached a new level of extreme tension.

Chapter 17

What About Justice?

CARMICHAEL'S AND KING'S SPEECHES HAD a profound impact on Wallace and many of his classmates. While previously many black students were hesitant to talk about the racism they encountered, in the wake of Impact, they began to speak honestly about their common experiences.

"We admitted that while many people were the finest of people, the overwhelming number of students and many others either ignored us or were hostile," Wallace said in a speech decades later. "You must know that the impact of this realization on many of us was devastating. What about the promise of equality? Of opportunity? Of justice?"

It wasn't as if all this came as a complete shock to Wallace. As a high school senior, he gave Vanderbilt "the hardest look" that he could. But that hard look, he began to realize, had been through a lens made narrow by circumstances beyond his control. He had been looking from a distance. From segregation. Through the eyes of a seventeen-year-old. Now his eyes were opening, his lens widening, but much of what became visible was ugly.

"Even if you grew up in segregation, you would hear the national anthem and hear about the Constitution, and there was all this talk about equality and fairness and justice," he recalled. "And there were beginning to be overt, explicit kinds of comments and statements that said, 'Come out and live in America and have equal opportunity like everybody else.' But what happened in reality was that sometimes that was true and sometimes it wasn't. You really hoped that America was not just someplace that plays a cruel joke on you. We were on campus and had our hopes and dreams like everybody else, and what we were seeing was that in coming into mainstream America, there were some disappointing things, some disappointing realities that were rather harsh. And we discovered that we needed to pull together."

There was an alternative to banding together that also carried appeal, and that was to remove oneself from the situation. It would be a lot easier to leave Vanderbilt than to change it. As the end of the school year approached, Wallace and Dillard broached this subject with Vanderbilt *Hustler* columnist Paul Kurtz. In what must have been a startling passage for Coach

Skinner and Chancellor Heard to read, Kurtz asked Wallace and Dillard: "Knowing what you know now, would you make the decision to come to Vanderbilt again?"

Perry declined to answer, while Dillard would only reply, "I've learned a lot about the South since I've come to Vanderbilt and would think seriously about making the same decision."

The article caught the attention of the head of Vanderbilt's administration, Chancellor Heard, who scribbled off a note to his dean of students.

Can anything be done to help with this? he asked.

It was here in the spring of 1967 that a disheartened Wallace was as close to giving up on Vanderbilt as he ever would be. Coming off a freshman season in which he averaged twenty points and seventeen rebounds per game, he appeared destined for stardom when he joined the varsity. But the troubling truth was that dealing with the isolation on campus and the hostile gyms on the road for another season, and then two more insanely stressful years on top of that, was more than Wallace had bargained for, more painful than he cared to endure.

The combined weight of the shocking mistreatment he'd experienced, the broken promise of equality he'd been dismayed to discover on campus, and the general anxiety of college life was threatening to crush him.

While Dillard's predicament was similar to Wallace's, there

was one key difference: he began to sense—a telling comment here, a dismissive action there—that while the administration and coaching staff were invested in Wallace's success, he, the brash black kid from the North, was becoming expendable—unnecessary and unwanted.

For both Wallace and Dillard, their interest in transferring to other colleges was genuine. Skinner read Kurtz's article and immediately summoned Wallace to his office. He told him he hoped he would stay at Vanderbilt and asked why Perry had not mentioned anything about this before.

"I had enough of a sense of dedication and responsibility than to bring up all of these problems in the midst of a season when we're trying to win games," Wallace recalled. "That wasn't responsible or fair to the university or the coaches. But after the season—that's what that period was about."

Following Wallace's meeting with the coach, he and Dillard talked it over, and in addition to a lengthy list of reasons to transfer, they both recognized compelling reasons to stay.

"We both knew the symbolic reasons why we were there," Dillard said, "and even though we wanted to quit, we wanted to leave, it was just like, 'We can't do that; we just have to tough it out.'"

While Wallace and others experienced difficulties on campus strong enough to cause them to question their decisions to attend Vanderbilt, there remained pockets of support among some white professors and administrators.

One such ally was Reverend Bev Asbury, the university chaplain, who invited Wallace and several other black students to his office to talk about their day-to-day experiences. The discussion was so chilling that Asbury asked the students whether they'd like to come to his home to talk further.

"I just asked, 'What has your first year at Vanderbilt been like?' and their answers were just stunning," Asbury recalled. He heard stories of signs placed on dormitory doors reading *Nigger go home*. Confederate flags and swastikas, too. Walter Murray told the story of his profane welcome to English class. Bedford Waters told Asbury that black students "were torn because you wanted to be a part of the campus, and you also wanted to bond with the other African American students, and yet there was a perception that if a group of us were together, there was going to be a race riot or something."

As Asbury sat and listened to these stories, he was struck by the courage it took for these "normal kids" simply to exist at Vanderbilt. Helping them was why he had come to the university in the first place, and he knew one man who needed to hear their stories.

"All these reports went on, and I listened and listened," Asbury recalled. "And then I said, 'Would you like the opportunity to tell the chancellor all of this?' And they said, 'Yes, we would; nobody has heard our story.' And so I picked up the phone and called Chancellor Heard that night."

With a week to prepare for the meeting with Heard, the students thought carefully about what they would say and who should serve as the leader of the delegation. Even most of the older students sensed there was just one option. The question was whether the freshman, Perry Wallace, would accept.

He did.

Climbing the stairs outside Kirkland Hall, Perry Wallace appeared so calm that the students following him gained confidence with each step. Wallace had performed in front of hostile crowds across the Deep South over the course of the season, had even lived through the hell of Starkville, Mississippi. He was six foot five, 220 pounds, and as smart as anyone on campus. This was a man to follow. And yet, here, in his hometown, on his own college campus, flanked by friends who admired him, and headed to a meeting with a man he respected, Perry Wallace felt one overwhelming sensation: "scared as hell."

Wallace was afraid because he understood how explosive this meeting could be: a dozen black students, walking into Chancellor Heard's office, sitting down with him and other administrators and daring to tell these older white men what was wrong with their university. The North Nashville riot was still fresh in everyone's minds; tensions in the city remained high. These kinds of encounters typically didn't end well, Wallace thought. Still, he knew this meeting was one of the most critical moments of his college experience, and more than that, he understood how important it was that he, the high-profile basketball star, not just be part of the group but lead it into the room.

Wallace spoke first, telling the administrators that the students simply wanted to explain—by relaying personal stories—what it was like to be black at Vanderbilt.

The esteemed English faculty? Might call you a nigger on your first day of class. Fraternities and sororities? Didn't mind hiring black bands on weekends, but wouldn't dare admit a black member. The dormitories? The kind of place where the father of a white student might protest his daughter's assigned roommate, if the roommate happened to be black. The freethinkers on campus? Often condescending, saying they supported blacks but doing very little to help conditions improve. The stories went on and on, all told in a matter-of-fact style.

As the session unfolded, the students sensed that their voices finally were being heard. The chancellor asked good questions, allowed the students to speak their minds, listened without judgment.

"All the black students had immense respect for Chancellor Heard," Wallace recalled. "He was not only a true intellectual, but he was a statesman. And in that sense, he did listen and he actually understood."

Up to this point, the chancellor's philosophy on integration at Vanderbilt had been based on a simple, seemingly logical plan: the university should treat the black students just like everybody else. That meant no segregated dorms or classes, but also no special orientation sessions, no black fraternities or sororities, no black student association, no black history classes. As the students' stories made clear, this hands-off approach was not only ineffective, it was creating tremendous suffering. Paying no special attention to the school's first waves of black students, but then subjecting them to racist professors, hostile classmates, and a segregated social system was, it began to dawn on the chancellor, a form of cruel and unusual punishment.

At a gathering of university faculty the following fall, Heard explained the revelation he experienced while listening to Wallace, Dillard, and their classmates: "It seems to me that the principle on which we have been operating—that all Vanderbilt students shall be treated alike by Vanderbilt without regard to race or color—may have proved insufficient," he said. "We may be in the ironic position of needing to treat our Negro students differently in order to treat them equally—that is, in order to afford them a reasonable opportunity to gain a personal and educational experience equivalent in its general value to that we believe we afford to most other students."

For Wallace, the encounter with Heard was an empowering experience. Within the span of weeks, he had spoken frankly with the two most important authority figures in his life at Vanderbilt, Skinner and Heard. He had experienced the worst of human nature in the South and knew that this had just been a warm-up act, a freshman season that wouldn't even register in the record books. His first year of varsity ball—and all the torment that would surely come with it—was still six months away.

When he made the decision to attend Vanderbilt, it had been a naïve one, but now he knew exactly what he was in for. "I knew what could be bad about it. I knew I didn't like it," Wallace said. "I knew that change wasn't going to happen overnight. And I knew that if I stayed, I'd be making a commitment to making some change, and that I'd have to fight the battles to make it happen."

It was a shift in Wallace's mind-set that would change his life forever, giving his every action a higher purpose. "I hadn't really embraced the situation I had placed myself in, because I hadn't known what it really meant. I hadn't really said to myself, 'This is what you've agreed to do, to try to help work for change.' But in the spring of 1967, it finally congealed.

"This," Wallace recalled, "is when I finally became a real pioneer."

Chapter 18

The Invisible Man

COMMODORE SUPER FANS MORRIS MORGAN and Henry Robinson were hiding in the shadows in the back of the gym when they saw it happen.

Forty years later, Morgan could still picture the scene in his mind's eye: Godfrey Dillard quickly flashing down the court on his way to the hoop. A defender darts across the court to cut him off, so Dillard plants on his left leg, a quick stop to allow him take the ball to the basket. *Boooom!* Dillard's left knee buckles, and Morgan is stunned as he watches his friend collapse in pain on the hardwood. "My knee, my knee!" Dillard yells.

Morgan looked on as Perry Wallace rushed over and helped Dillard to his feet, pulled an arm over his shoulder, and walked him back to the locker room.

The next day, Wallace and his teammates arrived at Memorial Gym and slipped on their uniforms, lining up in two rows for the team picture. This was the history-making shot, the first time an African American appeared with a varsity SEC basketball team. In the middle of the second row, there was Perry Wallace, the lone black face. Because he was injured, Dillard was not invited to pose for the camera.

1967-68 VANDERBILT UNIVERSITY BASKETBALL

Hal Bartch Bob Bundy Godfrey Dillard Dan Due Tom Hagan

Gene Lockyear Perry Wallace Bob Warren Art Welhoelter Bo Wyenandt

In this publicity slick created before the 1967–68 season, Godfrey Dillard is still depicted as a member of the varsity. He would injure his knee during an October 31 practice and never play a varsity game.

VANDERBILT UNIVERSITY ATHLETIC DEPARTMENT.

"Once again, it was fate," Dillard said years later. "The picture; I'm not in it. I was becoming invisible."

Less than twenty-four hours before that photo was taken, Wallace and Dillard had blazed down the court together. But Wallace had walked off it, inching closer to his place in history, while Dillard limped away, speeding toward obscurity. Two steps forward, one step back; as with so many things on the Vanderbilt campus that fall, change was happening, the 1960s were finally arriving, but only in fits and starts.

More than one Vanderbilt student described the campus mood in the fall of 1967 as like "an awakening," a time when it was dawning on many white students that black people wished to be treated as equals. The first tentative efforts to do so were often painfully awkward.

The fact that Wallace was so well spoken was seen as a novelty by some of his friends, leading to embarrassing and dehumanizing moments for Wallace. As if encouraging a baby to smile for a photograph, one of Wallace's white classmates begged Wallace to talk—just say something, anything!—when the student's parents visited campus. The encounter made Wallace feel as though he were being treated like a circus act.

While a handful of white students had attended integrated high schools, most had grown up in environments in which the idea of interacting on equal footing with blacks was a foreign concept. Bob Warren, Wallace's teammate from rural Kentucky, had encountered just two black people in his entire life before enrolling at Vanderbilt and meeting Wallace.

And for every student like Warren, there were others like Marshall Chapman at the other extreme—constant exposure, but still no equality. The daughter of a white South Carolina cotton mill owner, Chapman had been raised by black women.

"I grew up with so many blacks in the house, bathing you, dressing you, combing your hair, cooking all the food you ate," she recalled. "There are home movies of us in Florida, and they break your heart in the way my grandfather was only interested in his grandchildren. So there are all these little towheaded blond white children [holding on to] these black arms, and you never saw their faces. That kind of says it all."

Even small attempts at bridging these cultural gaps were too much for some students and parents to stomach. One father, having read about the plight of Vanderbilt's black students in the Vanderbilt *Hustler*, was sufficiently enraged to write a letter to the paper.

"So far I have received three copies and each one has an article about the poor, mistreated, misunderstood nigger," wrote W. L. Sefton of Jacksonville, Florida. "I happen to be one person who is sick and tired of seeing nothing but nigger trouble on TV and reading [the] same in every paper one picks up. If each issue of your publication is going to have articles defending these people, just take my name off your mailing list."

Among the school's biggest boosters, wealthy people who donated money to Vanderbilt, the backlash took subtler forms. Nashville businessman Joel Gordon heard members of Vanderbilt's Board of Trust say that they would boycott Commodore games to protest Wallace's presence.

Despite the pressure from outside, Walter Murray and several of his black classmates sensed that many administrators and faculty members were committed to improving campus life for black students, but the problem, Murray told a *Hustler* reporter, was that "we don't live with the administration; we live with the student body, and that is where the ultimate change must come."

Speaking to a *Hustler* reporter, Wallace explained that even with good intentions, the administration's efforts were by their nature long-term approaches—a frustrating reality for students looking for change in their own lives. "We are interested in immediate action that will improve our college life while we are students here," he said.

Sparked to take action on their own terms, an Afro American student association began to crystallize in the fall of 1967.

"We are not going to sit back and be stagnant until the white student decides to hand us our freedom," Dillard said.

While waiting for the association to gain official university approval, the black students began to organize social gatherings on weekends. The hub of activity was a lounge on the eleventh floor of one of the Carmichael Towers dormitories. Morris Morgan turned the study lounge into a party room on Saturday nights. Morgan would carry his stereo system down the hall; students, including Wallace and Dillard, would bring their records; the lights would be turned down low; and the kids would hang out and dance. The lounge became so synonymous with black life on campus that when the students launched their own literary magazine, filled with poetry, essays, and other commentary on the black experience, they called it *Rap from the 11th Floor*.

While the black students gained confidence and began to organize, the university administration also took formal steps to address their concerns. In the meeting with the chancellor the previous spring, the idea of forming a "Human Relations Committee," a permanent race-relations council of students, faculty, and administrators, had been discussed. Conversations about such a group became more serious in the fall of 1967, and Wallace was given the power to call the group to order.

But first, he had a basketball league to desegregate.

Chapter 19

Slammed Shut

SPORTS ILLUSTRATED PICKED THE COMMODORES to win the SEC in the 1967–68 season.

Coach Skinner told the *Hustler* that this team was probably the best fast-breaking squad he'd ever coached.

If Perry Wallace had any notions of flying under the radar as he toured the South in his first year on the varsity, that wasn't going to be the case. All eyes were on the Commodores.

Skinner worried about a tough schedule—four of the first five opponents were ranked in the top twenty in the nation—and Dillard's injury left an already thin roster even thinner. It also meant that Wallace would be going it alone in his first varsity season.

Where would he now turn for support?

It wasn't the loss of his fellow trailblazer, however, that threatened the greatest disruption to Wallace's season; it was the loss of his favorite shot. Just three days after UCLA completed a perfect 30-0 season and won the 1967 national championship, a committee of coaches and administrators outlawed the slam dunk.

The "stuff shot" was Wallace's most reliable offensive move, the "freedom song" that had carried him from the playgrounds of North Nashville to the frenzied gym at Pearl High and across town to Vanderbilt. Now, just before he was to play his first varsity game, that song had been silenced.

While the ban wasn't explicitly directed at Wallace, it was more than just a coincidence that the rules of the game changed just as the first black player—a prolific dunker—was about to enter the league that Kentucky coach Adolph Rupp had dominated for decades. If the rabid crowd in Starkville had demonstrated a raw, emotional reaction to the emergence of blacks in the game, the coaches and administrators who banned the dunk were equally motivated by race—erasing a form of Black Power with the stroke of a pen to the rule books.

As William Rhoden wrote in *Forty Million Dollar Slaves*, this wasn't the first time that the "level playing field of sport" had been tilted. "Black athletes across the board have been faced with ever-changing rules designed to maintain white dominance," he wrote. "Mostly this has meant using power to change the rules of engagement."

In the NFL, after R. C. Owens of the Baltimore Colts

blocked a field goal by leaping above the goalpost's crossbar, a rule was changed to prevent such maneuvers. In basketball, the dominant play of big men such as Wilt Chamberlain and Bill Russell led to the widening of the foul lane and the creation of offensive goaltending.

While the national media then—and in years since—have attributed the ban solely to the dominance of black UCLA center Lew Alcindor, the legendary NBA player who later changed his name to Kareem Abdul-Jabbar, an entirely believable theory is that Perry Wallace had as much to do with the ban as anyone.

While Rupp was no longer on the rules committee when the dunk was banned, he had been the committee's most powerful member for many years prior and still held great sway. David Lattin had embarrassed Rupp's Wildcats with a powerful dunk in the 1966 NCAA title game. The next season, Lattin's protégé, Wallace, embarrassed Rupp's freshman team with a slam of his own. Kentucky didn't have UCLA on its schedule, but it did have to play Vanderbilt twice a year.

"When you look back, you see it was a silly, suspicious rule, and I think it said a whole lot about the times," Wallace said.

Looking back on the ban from the distance of decades, Skinner agreed. "Oh my God, it made me just sick for [Perry] when they banned the dunk," he said. "I was for the dunk and was really opposed to the no-dunk rule. Rupp and a few of them scattered around were against it. Rupp was a big part of it because the dunk was hurting him. It took away Perry's game. When he first came [to Vanderbilt], Perry couldn't do anything but dunk and rebound. The ban forced him to become a basketball player."

Wallace agrees with that assessment, but he also found the silver lining in a suspicious rule by saying that the prohibition of the dunk compelled him to work on his skills farther away from the basket. It was something he'd need to do anyway if he wanted to play at the next level. There weren't many six-five centers in the NBA.

Wallace believed there was another benefit to the ban: a reduced chance of injury. Despite his ability to leap high into the air to throw down rim-rattling dunks, the joy he took in these jams was tempered by fear. In a junior high school game, Wallace had jumped up to block a shot, only to have the shooter "low-bridge" him, clipping his legs and causing him to land flat on his back. Though he played through the pain and finished the game, Wallace went to bed that night feeling a strange sensation in his back and legs. When he woke up the next morning, he could not move. His mother asked why he was still in bed, and Wallace pretended he had a cold. Unable to stand, he crawled to the bathroom when no one was looking.

"I had some paralysis," Wallace recalled. "That period where I could not walk had a huge impact on me. I tried to work my way back by doing exercises and stretching and that sort of stuff, and the feeling gradually came back. But that whole episode taught me about playing defensively; still being a leaper, but playing defensively."

Having played through rough games as a freshman, Wallace knew he'd be even more of a target during his first year on the varsity. His freedom song had been silenced, but he tried to focus on the one positive aspect of the situation: a rule change designed to limit him might actually serve to protect him. "By having the dunk outlawed," he said, "I didn't have to leap to try to dunk and create a situation where people could physically really do me in." The unintended consequence of the ban meant he would be a little bit safer.

But that did not mean he would be safe.

Chapter 20

As Good as It Gets

First came Samantha, the hobbling basset hound and unofficial team mascot. Then the pep band struck up "Dynamite," the Vandy fight song, and the fans roared. The cheerleaders, hand in hand in a V formation like a flock of birds, came charging out onto the court. And then came the Commodore players, jogging through a small doorway, and the crowd grew louder still.

Public-address announcer Herman Grizzard introduced the visiting Auburn Tigers, and each player was met with a round of boos as he ran out to midcourt to shake hands with the Commodore mascot. Then it was time to meet the Vanderbilt starters—Bo Wyenandt, Bob Warren, Kenny Campbell, Tom Hagan, and Perry Wallace—and the crowd greeted their boys with pent-up gusto, this being the first home game of the 1967–68 season.

It was now 7:30 p.m. on Monday, December 4, 1967. Time for tip-off, time for Perry Wallace to play his first game at Memorial Gym as a member of the Commodore varsity and his first varsity game against a Southeastern Conference opponent.

For there to be a Shaquille O'Neal at LSU, a Charles Barkley at Auburn, a John Wall at Kentucky, a Dominique Wilkins at Georgia, or a Joakim Noah at Florida, there first had to be this moment in the winter of 1967, Wallace leading the way for all those who would follow. He walked to midcourt and leaped high for the jump ball that began the game, soaring into the air right where Martin Luther King and Stokely Carmichael had stood eight months earlier.

Vanderbilt fans expected greatness from their Commodores, and they expected big things from Wallace. While he still had a lot to learn offensively, especially now that the dunk had been taken away, he had dominated games as a defender and rebounder as a freshman, and his early work prior to the home opener was encouraging. In the annual freshman-versus-varsity scrimmage in November, Wallace had been the most productive player on the court, leading the varsity with eighteen points and twelve rebounds. In the season opener December 2, a road game at Southern

Methodist University, Wallace collected ten rebounds, and Vanderbilt won in overtime, 88–84.

Yet there was cause for some concern among the Commodore faithful, as the team just barely earned the victory against the inferior Mustangs. Then the Auburn game did little to ease their worries. Though Auburn was clearly overmatched, the Tigers forced a sloppy and rough style of play against the Commodores, and Vanderbilt never got its smooth, fast-break style into high gear. In all, the referees whistled a total of forty-four fouls.

Whistles everywhere, it seemed, except in one of the most obvious cases.

Wallace had played tentatively against SMU, careful not to accidentally throw an elbow or shove a player and set off a fight. Playing in front of the home crowd, he felt more comfortable against Auburn. But then he took a flagrant karate chop to the back, and the crowd howled as the referees let the game continue with no foul called against Auburn's Wally Tinker. For Wallace, the incident was a shocking introduction to the treatment he would frequently receive from players and referees alike over the course of the season.

"After that [blow]," Wallace told a Vanderbilt *Hustler* reporter a few months later, "I was always a bit leery." Just one incident in one ball game, but a telling glimpse into the dangers of pioneering.

Just before Tinker hit him, Wallace had blocked his shot, sending the ball flying. "No doubt he was embarrassed and angered at this 'black block,'" Wallace said. "So, yes, Wally and the boys were pissed—but they were also intimidated, and by a black."

Back in the Vanderbilt huddle immediately after Tinker's hack job, Wallace collected his thoughts, pondering the likely outcomes if he retaliated. How could he "get back at" Wally Tinker and get away with it? Would Vanderbilt fans support him if he engaged in aggression against a white player? How would Tiger fans treat him when Vandy traveled to Auburn?

"These questions were real to me, and I had no choice but to act accordingly," Wallace recalled, ultimately deciding that the best way to get back at Auburn was to play his hardest and win the game. "That may not have been clear to many people. Some blacks called my reaction weak, and some whites who congratulated me for my 'character' were just phonies who were happy to avoid dealing with race and who really didn't care if a black suffered."

(And a postscript to the Tinker story: About twenty years later, at an SEC event where Wallace was honored, he ran into a gracious Wally Tinker. "After we had talked a few minutes, he did an amazing thing," Wallace said. "He related that he had heard about how that famous blow had affected me, and he apologized. I accepted, and we continued to chat like old

Wallace's leaping ability and court sense made him one of Vanderbilt's all-time greatest rebounders. He ended his career with 849 rebounds, ranking second in school history.

friends—two men, two Southerners, two Americans. He had reflected and America had begun to change. I call that a victory, a much greater and transformative one than 'getting' Wally Tinker.")

Despite Tinker's blow, Wallace's SEC debut was successful, as Vanderbilt won, 78–65, and improved to 2-0, good enough for a number eight national ranking.

In the moments after the game, however, Skinner was concerned. If his team continued to play this sloppily, he worried, they'd be 2-3 in a matter of days. On their way to Nashville over the course of just eight days were North Carolina, Davidson, and Duke, three powerhouses from one state, all nationally ranked.

"I can't remember three tougher games in a row," Skinner said.

For Wallace, the three-game stretch would be especially gratifying. After playing as a freshman in cracker-box gyms at schools that cared a lot more about football than basketball, this, he believed, was big-time basketball. And, more meaningfully, each of the teams coming to Memorial would bring along a pioneer of its own. Charlie Scott at North Carolina, Mike Maloy at Davidson, and C. B. Claiborne at Duke were each the first black players to play for those universities, adding to the list of black stars who appeared in Memorial Gymnasium in 1967.

First up were the Tar Heels, ranked fifth in the country. Energized by an uncommonly lively crowd, even by Memorial Gym standards, Vanderbilt eliminated the sloppy play that had plagued it against SMU and Auburn, getting its fast-break game into high gear and crashing the boards to collect key rebounds against the bigger, stronger North Carolina team. The style of play was especially rough for Wallace, banging around under the basket with the larger Tar Heel players. At one point, he took a hard shot directly to the nose.

Vanderbilt led by seven points at halftime, the crowd's screams bouncing off the Memorial Gym cinder blocks with such force as the first-half clock expired that two Vandy players said their ears were still ringing when they reached the locker room.

In the second half, Skinner pulled Vanderbilt forward Bo Wyenandt away from the basket when Vanderbilt had the ball, drawing his defender with him, unclogging the lane for fellow forward Bob Warren, who led the way with eighteen points, and guard Tom Hagan, who scored sixteen of his eighteen points in the half. UNC's full-court press was ineffective, and with Hagan leading the way, the Commodores were nearly unstoppable, hitting on eighteen of twenty-eight field goals and twenty of twenty-two free throws in the second half. Vanderbilt won, 89–76.

Yet in the locker room, Wallace, rubbing the bridge of his nose, was perplexed: a distressing trend was emerging. "I believe [my nose] is broken," he said. "Why is it every time one of the big centers turns toward the basket, his elbow catches me in the nose?"

Not only had Wallace taken a blow to the face, he'd also been targeted by the referees, drawing his fourth foul early in the second half.

Skinner heard Wallace's lament but offered little consolation. "You have to learn to duck," he said, yet another episode where Wallace didn't receive the support he needed from his teammates and coaches.

Despite the bittersweet taste the UNC game left in Wallace's mouth, good news arrived on campus in the form of the next national poll, which after the Carolina victory listed the Commodores at number three in the country, trailing only top-ranked UCLA, led by Alcindor, and number two Houston. With undefeated, number eight–ranked Davidson on the way to town, anticipation for the game reached a fever pitch.

While Skinner downplayed his team's chances, Davidson coach Lefty Driesell talked up his team's talents without hesitation. "My best ever," he said. If anyone could snap Vanderbilt's thirty-two-game nonconference home winning streak, Driesell believed he had the team to do it. And just after halftime, it appeared as though Driesell might be right: Davidson had a thirteen-point lead.

But Vanderbilt whittled the Wildcat lead down to three points with three minutes to go. It was at that point, Driesell said later, that his players began to force bad shots under pressure. The Commodores tied the score, and Hagan had a chance to win the game in regulation but missed a jumper as time expired, sending the game into overtime.

In the extra session, Wallace controlled a jump ball with ninety seconds remaining and the score tied, and Vanderbilt held the ball for one final shot. Once again, Hagan took the big shot with the game on the line—his one-handed jumper hit nothing but net and sent students flooding onto the court. Rising above all the commotion was a student waving a crutch—a joyful Godfrey Dillard in the center of it all.

Two powerhouses defeated, one more—Duke—left to go. Heading into the third and final leg of the gauntlet, one thing out of Skinner's control was the health of his players. Warren had injured a leg against Davidson, but more troubling was a citywide flu epidemic that was threatening to decimate his team. (It was only much later that several players discovered that they had actually been struck with mononucleosis, an illness that limited their strength and stamina for much of the season.)

"Even if they get out [of bed] before game time, they'll be rubbery-legged and unable to go full speed for any length of time," Skinner worried. "I'm no doctor, but I'm afraid they'll not be in first-class shape to play against a team as good as Duke."

With Hagan picking up four quick fouls, Duke led by as many as eleven points in the first half, took a 44–37 lead into halftime, and extended the lead back to ten points over the first several minutes of the second half.

But just as it appeared that the Commodores would succumb to Duke and the flu, a last-gasp burst of energy appeared out of nowhere. Wallace outmuscled Duke's front line for rebound after rebound, collecting a season-high fifteen by game's end. Hagan shook off his foul trouble to begin pouring in points. Wyenandt forgot about his illness and started draining jumpers. Over an eight-minute stretch midway through the second half, Vanderbilt outscored the Blue Devils 19–7 to take the lead.

The crowd was raucous, an improbable victory close at hand, but then a whistle with just over two minutes left. The fifth, disqualifying foul was called on Hagan, who was leading the team with twenty-six points. Boos came cascading down from the balconies, and then students began hurling ice cubes onto the floor in protest. A referee signaled toward the Vanderbilt bench.

Skinner got up from his chair and walked, head down, toward the scorer's table. He grabbed the microphone. "We've got a chance to win this game," he calmly told the crowd. "If you continue to throw stuff out here, you can cost us a technical foul and the game. Please help us."

The lead seesawed in the final seconds, Duke recovering from a 74–70 deficit to take a 75–74 lead with seventeen seconds left. One final possession for Vanderbilt. With Hagan on the bench, it would be up to Wyenandt to take the game winner. He dribbled into the corner of the court but was cut off by Duke defenders. A quick pass, then the ball returned to Wyenandt just above the foul circle. A couple of dribbles to collect himself, and he let loose from twenty-five feet. Bucket! Ball game. More pandemonium.

At this moment, more than at any other time since he had meditated on that rock and decided to attend Vanderbilt, Wallace felt at peace with his decision to become a Commodore. From a basketball perspective, things could not be better.

Was it too good to be true?

Chapter 21

The Sudden Fall

No one could have anticipated that Commodore basketball had arrived at a precipice from which it would almost immediately descend. Five games into his varsity career, Wallace had experienced the best it would ever get. It all started with a queasy feeling in his stomach after the Duke game. The mono bug had caught up with him.

The first signs of the team's fall were evident in the locker room at the University of Florida. It was halftime of Vanderbilt's first game since the win over Duke, and although Vanderbilt led the Gators 44–30, the ominous signals were hard to miss. First, the room was emptier than it should have been. Assistant Coach Garr was in bed back in Nashville, too sick with the flu to make the trip. More important, Bob Warren, who had spent the morning soaking in a whirlpool, had been left behind at the hotel, hobbling on crutches and nursing injuries to his wrist, shoulder, and leg. Just a few days removed from a 102-degree fever that kept him out of the Duke game, guard Kenny Campbell slumped in his chair, sick as a dog.

Florida opened the second half with an aggressive pressing defense, wearing Campbell down and forcing a series of Vanderbilt turnovers. Little by little, the Commodores' lead drifted away, and when the clock hit :00, the scoreboard read Florida 74, Vanderbilt 72.

As team manager Gene Smitherman collected sweaty uniforms in the locker room, he felt the outcome represented more than just one loss; it punctured the team's self-confidence. "It was a bad letdown," he recalled. "I had been in awe over our wins against Duke, Davidson, and North Carolina, because frankly I didn't know we were that good. And then here was a sign that we may not have been."

In the wake of more losses to Kentucky and Tennessee, the mood on campus grew sour, the conventional wisdom holding that the season, with nearly two months still left to go, was effectively over. Some fans pinned their frustrations on Wallace, calling for him to be more assertive.

Wallace said he heard the complaints from both the black and white communities—two sides of the same coin. From white fans came jeers urging him to mix it up under the boards. *You're not aggressive enough, Wallace! You're lazy! Jump, boy, jump!* Some black observers felt that Wallace was overly deferential in his new surroundings and urged him to let loose and take more shots.

To say that Wallace considered himself in a no-win situation is an understatement. First, because he was suffering from mono, he simply wasn't able to jump and run as he normally could. Second, there was an extra level of hesitation to his game for two reasons: he imposed some of it on himself in an effort to avoid starting a fight in which he knew he'd be outnumbered, and there was the growing uncertainty he began to feel when officials overlooked the cheap shots thrown his way. Third, Wallace resisted the calls to shoot more often for the most logical of reasons: he knew he simply wasn't very good at it. His best offensive move, the dunk, had been taken away.

Whatever the reason, Wallace felt his portion of the blame came with an extra dose of disdain. "I'm not saying it was all racial; some of it was just the frustration of the people who were screaming," Wallace recalled. "But I am saying the parts where they're saying, 'Nigger, you better jump!' I guarantee you it's hard to take race out of that. Some of these people were really nasty, and my parents had to hear some of that stuff. There were some games where I didn't play well, there's no question about that, but some of these people weren't able

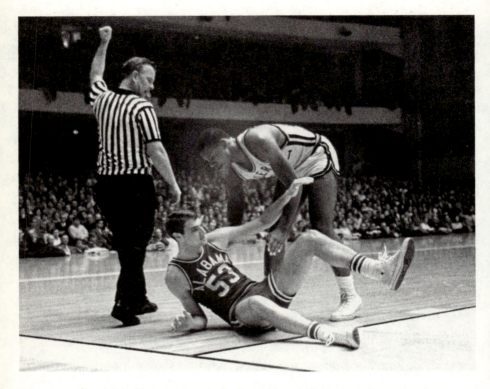

Conscious of how his actions on the court could be perceived by teammates, opponents, and fans, Wallace limited his aggressiveness to prevent accidental blows that could ignite fights.

PHOTO BY ROBERT JOHNSON, THE TENNESSEAN.

to apply an ordinary level of criticism. They were foaming at the mouth and took it right to the bottom. The words you heard people use [on our home court] were the same ones you heard down in Mississippi or Alabama."

Wallace played through the criticism, and in the aftermath,

he'd hear from old friends and acquaintances from his neigh-borhood or over at Tennessee State University (as the all-black Tennessee A&I was officially renamed that year), not with words of encouragement but with another brand of con-demnation, disparaging his decision to attend Vanderbilt. He shouldn't be playing with those white boys, they'd say; he should have gone to a black college.

"You'd have black people—sometimes with college degrees—saying, 'You ought to get the ball, take more shots, be more confrontational, to hell with them white boys.' Think of what those people didn't understand," Wallace recalled. "Those peo-ple had no idea what I was doing. Do you know I'm helping to integrate the SEC? The only way I could have done what I did was to have a measure of real restraint—because at the same time I'm really pushing the envelope. I'm doing it in a way that you call nonthreatening, but it creates a real possibility to get it done. I couldn't do it with a clenched fist."

Chapter 22

Nightmares

WHEN A VANDERBILT MAGAZINE DESCRIBED life on the road for the 1968 Commodore basketball team, it must have sounded like a dream come true to students, what with the chartered planes, fine motels, and catered meals. For most players, these trips were exciting adventures and highly anticipated departures from the ordinary.

But nothing illustrated the very different worlds in which Perry Wallace and the rest of his teammates existed than the emotions evoked by these swings through the small towns of the SEC. For all but one Commodore, road trips were about trying to win a game and having some fun; for Wallace, they were about survival. The very idea of traveling south was a source of enormous stress for the league's only black player,

and the trips themselves were variations on the theme that began in Starkville the year before—the stuff of nightmares.

In a *Sports Illustrated* article on Vanderbilt's quick start, Curry
Kirkpatrick wrote that of the four pioneers who would play
at Memorial Gym that season (Wallace, Maloy, Claiborne,
and Scott), it was Wallace, facing journeys to the "deep, deep
South," who would confront the toughest challenge.

Drawing upon his own life experiences and what he knew
of the collective black experience in the South, Wallace approached the team's upcoming three-game road trip to Alabama, Mississippi, and Louisiana with what he later described
as "the deepest sense of dread." No one had ever done what
he was doing before, and no one in the traveling party could
relate to what he was feeling. He dreamed of the worst that
could happen and took deliberate steps to avoid such a fate.
And in Wallace's mind, the worst that could happen was getting shot and killed, either on the court or around town before
a game.

Wallace's teammate Bill LaFevor remembered a scene at a
Mississippi movie theater. "About two or three minutes before the movie was over, somebody behind me mentioned
that Perry had gotten up and gone out of the theater," he
said. "When the movie was over, we all went back to the cars,
and Perry was there waiting for us. My feeling was that he
realized it had gotten dark and that he was in Mississippi.

There was a saying: 'Nigger, don't let the sun set on [you] in Mississippi.' We went to the theater when it was light, and while we were watching the movie, it got dark. And he was out there trying to get into that car. It was locked and he couldn't get in, and he was concerned about it. And looking back on it now, realistically concerned about it."

Wallace remembers the scene well. "I was concerned about a 'failure to communicate' between me and some Mississippi bigots," he recalled. "What I had thought was a relatively tiny, 'safe' little movie theater was apparently actually a popular Friday-night attraction for the community—the white community. I knew my teammates meant well, but I also knew that they hadn't a single clue. I had to provide for my own protection."

Whenever his teammates departed for dinner on this three-game swing to Auburn, Mississippi State, and Louisiana State, Wallace chose to stay in his room, telling the others that he had a stomachache or needed to stay in and study. "I remember in Starkville, he would not go out to dinner with us," Wyenandt said. "We could not talk him into going. We were like, 'Come on, Perry,' but he was not going to go out of that room."

On most nights, Wallace remained in his room alone, but occasionally he had company. Bob Warren, the straight-arrow forward from Hardin, Kentucky, whose prior experience with blacks was limited to childhood encounters with a black-smith and a maid, was assigned to room with Wallace on a number of trips. Feeling challenged academically at Vanderbilt, Warren often used his free time to study. Warren said he and Wallace spent many nights reading until they turned out the lights.

But when the lights came back on, it was once again time to step onto a hostile court. Emotions were especially intense whenever Vanderbilt traveled to Knoxville to take on the rival Tennessee Vols. From opposing fans and cheerleaders alike came the most vile of epithets, from the pregame warm-ups to the final buzzer:

Nigger!

Jigaboo!

Charcoal!

Coon!

We're gonna lynch you, boy!

The words rained down on Wallace, but that wasn't all. He was spit on and pelted with Cokes, ice, and coins.

It was one thing to withstand a bout of insults, no matter how harsh, but it was another thing entirely to receive death threats. At LSU, in a heated matchup against the Tigers, Wallace never actually felt the bite of a blade, but some Vanderbilt players claimed a dagger was thrown on the court in his direction.

During a trip to Knoxville, the fans tried to wrestle Wallace's attention away from the game with a chilling sight: up in the stands, folks dangled a noose near the Vanderbilt bench, pretending they were threatening to hang Wallace.

Unlike the incident in the Duke game when Skinner took the microphone to plead with Vanderbilt fans to quit throwing ice on the floor, there were no such calls for respect when Wallace was the target on the road. While Chancellor Heard was coming to the conclusion that in order for blacks to have the same positive experience on campus as white students, they'd have to be treated differently, Skinner had not had the same epiphany. Treating Wallace the same as the rest of his teammates meant no talks with the team about what Wallace was encountering on the road, no pleas for the team to band together in support of one of their own.

Wallace was alarmed and deeply saddened by the fact that his teammates and coaches proceeded as if nothing was wrong. Despite being surrounded by a sea of people, both friend and foe, it felt as though he were utterly alone.

Yet Wallace refused to let the threatening behavior destroy him. Though he feared for his life, Wallace persevered, understanding that though his tormenters wanted him to feel small, their misguided, hateful actions in fact revealed him to be the bigger man.

"These [fans] claimed to be good Americans," Wallace said,

Wallace blocks the shot of "Pistol Pete" Maravich, the high-scoring LSU sensation and NBA Hall of Famer.

PHOTO BY FRANK EMPSON, THE TENNESSEAN.

"yet they were viciously attacking a fellow American's right to 'life, liberty, and the pursuit of happiness.' They also claimed to be good Christians, yet one couldn't call their reactions to me acts of 'Christian love.' Finally, people like these believed they were racially 'superior,' yet their behavior wouldn't have qualified as even minimally 'civilized.' So, they failed at all of their most fundamental claims about themselves, while I embodied quite well the first two—which after all are the only valid ones."

Wallace has always gone to great lengths to say that he holds no hard feelings toward his teammates, saying that they were decent kids doing the best they could, having had no more experience with trailblazing than he had. Still, Wallace says, "The facts were dramatic, even poignant, and they certainly beg the question: why the hell didn't anyone ever say anything—or do anything—about the nightmarish things goings on?"

Earlier in the season, when Vanderbilt had beaten North Carolina, Davidson, and Duke, Wallace had been part of the greatest three-game stretch in the history of Vanderbilt basketball. By January 29, when the Commodores had beaten LSU to sweep the three-game Deep South road trip, Wallace—a solitary young pioneer thrust into a tempest of hate—had endured arguably the most emotionally taxing stretch of games any African American had ever experienced in American sports.

He'd seen the worst of human nature and felt lucky to be alive.

Again, he asked himself the question that had haunted him for weeks: What's the worst thing that could happen?

The answer was right there on the Vanderbilt schedule. February 10, 1968: at Ole Miss.

Chapter 23

Hate, Defeated

HE THOUGHT IT WOULD BRING him some comfort.

On the morning of Friday, February 9, 1968, the day Wallace and his teammates left for Mississippi to play against Ole Miss, he stopped by Pearl High to see old friends and to gain strength for the journey south. Instead, walking down the hallway of his old school, he was startled by the taunts of an older female staff member.

"Perry Wallace, you're nothing but a token," she said. "Those white folks are just using you and you're allowing it to happen."

While Wallace eventually discovered that the woman's barbs were rooted in jealousy (her son, an athlete, was not being recruited by Vanderbilt), her words—delivered in a building that had previously only brought warm feelings—added to his state of anxiety as he prepared for the trip.

This encounter was the first episode of what Perry Wallace later termed "Four Days in Hell," a series of events so emotionally and mentally devastating, he didn't speak of them for more than forty-five years.

Back in high school, when he was taking the first flights of his life and enjoying the attention lavished upon him by college recruiters, Perry Wallace experienced the unlikeliest of conversations while walking down the aisle of one particular plane.

A middle-aged man recognized him and struck up a conversation. The man was a former high school sports star from Jackson, Tennessee. He had gone on to great success in college, becoming the finest all-around athlete in the history of his school, starring in baseball, basketball, and football. An injury cut short his professional football career, and now he was back at his alma mater, coaching basketball. When he spotted Wallace walking down the aisle, he introduced himself and casually asked the Pearl High star whether he would be interested in playing for him.

The man was Eddie Crawford from Ole Miss.

Two years later, as Wallace boarded Vanderbilt's flight to Mississippi, the idea of playing a single game in Oxford, let alone an entire career there, was fraught with a sense of danger unlike anything he had ever experienced. Wallace would be the first black player to take the court in front of the University of Mississippi's basketball fans, in a game that would take place six years after the riots that had accompanied James Meredith's enrollment as the first black student at Ole Miss. Bullet holes from the Meredith riot still pocked the campus's iconic Lyceum building as Wallace and his teammates arrived in Oxford.

If his worst nightmare were going to come true, Wallace thought, this was where it would happen.

Oxford, Mississippi, was where he'd be shot.

Once again, most of Wallace's teammates and coaches were oblivious to his fears. But student manager Paul Wilson was the rare member of the Vanderbilt entourage who seemed to understand. Having grown up in Jackson, Mississippi—attending a segregated high school that sent dozens of students to Ole Miss every year—Wilson had nevertheless been raised "not to hate." When Wallace joined the Commodores, Wilson said his concern for the plight of blacks evolved from a "struggle *they* were going through, to one *we* were going through. He was our teammate." Unbeknownst to Wallace, Wilson took two steps to try to prevent a nightmare like the one Perry had experienced in Starkville against Mississippi State.

First, in creating the travel itinerary for the trip, he assigned himself to be Wallace's roommate at the Holiday Inn. When the Commodores arrived at the hotel after driving in from the airport, Wilson was surprised to see several police cars: "I remembered the Meredith riots, so I had a real tense feeling. It had to be one hundred times worse for Perry."

Wilson's next wise and thoughtful decision was to help create a buffer zone around the Commodore bench to protect Wallace. In the days leading up to the game, Wilson called his old high school friend Steven Ammann, who had an open-minded view on race. The plan they hatched called for Ammann to assemble a group of like-minded Ole Miss students and snatch up tickets in the row immediately behind the Vanderbilt bench.

"I had a great deal of respect for what Perry Wallace was doing," Ammann said, "so our hope was to create a little distance, to put some people there who would be close to the scene and would not be verbally abusive. There's something inside of you at a moment like that that says, 'This should go right for this person.'"

Almost to a man, Wallace and his teammates can recall the scene when Wallace came running out on the court for the first time, white socks pulled up high, short black shorts and black jersey, VANDERBILT etched out in white-and-gold letters in a horseshoe shape above his number 25. In Starkville a year earlier, Wallace had clasped hands with Godfrey Dillard to gain strength to face the hostile crowd. In Oxford, he was on his own.

The jeers started the moment Wallace emerged from the tunnel, louder, more sustained, and uglier than any of the Commodores had heard since Starkville. But there was something different about the Ole Miss brand of abuse. The words themselves were ugly, but they were made far uglier by the carefree enthusiasm with which they were delivered.

For the next two hours, in his second day in hell, Wallace would serve as this crowd's entertainment.

As Wallace and his teammates shot around before the game started, Bob Warren noticed something he had never heard before in warm-ups: laughter. Every time Wallace missed a shot, fumbled a rebound, or made the slightest misstep, the Ole Miss fans at courtside exploded in delight. Every time Wallace made a shot, the crowd booed.

And in between, it was *Go home, nigger!*

We're gonna kill you, nigger!

We'll lynch you, boy!

The game hadn't even started yet, and already things were out of control. Perhaps worst of all for Wallace, he knew he would begin the game on the bench as a substitute. He'd just have to sit and wait for the inevitable: when Skinner summoned him into the game, the fans would be ready, and the barrage would begin anew.

Tip-off came as scheduled at 7:30 p.m., temperatures outside the Coliseum dipping to near freezing. Ammann and his friends settled into their seats behind the Vanderbilt bench, their plan to protect Wallace from the vilest elements of the crowd already an apparent failure. Wallace watched as the teams traded baskets, the underdog Rebels sticking close to Vanderbilt throughout the early going.

Finally, Wallace entered the game. "I checked into the game, and they raised holy hell," he recalled. "Every time I made a mistake, everybody clapped, everybody laughed." On both ends of the court, Wallace and his teammates felt that he was being bumped and bruised more than usual, enduring a physical style of play the referees overlooked.

Then it happened. A blow that came so fast, no one knows who threw the elbow. Struggling for a rebound, Wallace was struck underneath the left eye, knocked so hard in the head that he momentarily lost his vision and staggered to regain his footing. Neither ref whistled a foul, nor did they call a halt to the game to allow Wallace to be treated. Coach Skinner didn't call a time-out. The Ole Miss crowd cheered, rising to its feet in delight.

Wallace felt "fuzzy," but no matter how bad he was hurt, the one thing he was not going to do was leave the court. But as he regained his sight, he looked down and saw blood.

At the next dead ball, trainer Joe Worden came off the bench to check on Wallace and saw his eye swelling shut. He summoned team manager Wilson, asking him to help Wallace back to the locker room. As Wilson grabbed Wallace's arm and handed him an ice pack, the Mississippian heard the crowd still cheering, still laughing, still cursing "nigger." A father and son spat in their direction. Another fan yelled, "We're going to kill you!"

Forty years later, Wilson said that at that moment, his body was shaking, never having been so angry and embarrassed in his entire life. Not quite sure what to say to Wallace as they approached the tunnel to the locker room, he simply said, "I'm sorry, Perry."

Wallace, head held high in pride, kept on walking, looking straight ahead. "It's OK," he said.

The halftime buzzer sounded, Vanderbilt leading 41–35, and soon the rest of the team filed into the locker room. Worden checked on Wallace, but the minutes ran by quickly, and Wallace was left on the training table with a bag of ice as coaches, teammates, and managers returned to the court for the second half. Eye swollen and hands cold from the ice, Perry could hear the Ole Miss crowd react when his teammates returned to the court without him: *Did the nigger go home?*

Where's the nigger?

Did he quit?

Not one member of the Vanderbilt traveling party stayed behind to accompany Wallace back onto the court. As he walked toward the tunnel to return to the bench for the second half, he understood more clearly than ever that his journey as a pioneer was one that he would be making alone.

Steven Ammann had said he felt in his heart that a night like this "should go right" for a person in Wallace's situation, and perhaps Coach Skinner felt a similar calling, putting Wallace in the starting lineup to begin the second half. In the Hollywood rendition of what would happen next, Wallace would rise above the madness of the crowd, soar above the floor for every rebound, shake off another hard blow to the head, score one basket after another, and lead Vanderbilt to a convincing victory.

In real life, amazingly, he did all that, even with a swollen eye, and he also unleashed a perfect, left-handed behind-the-back pass on a fast break for an easy layup.

In his encounter with Ole Miss coach Crawford on an airplane two years earlier, Wallace posed a question: If I decide to go to Vanderbilt, what is the atmosphere going to be like in your arena? Crawford told him the Ole Miss fans would be hard on him, and Wallace's only remedy would be to tune out the hecklers and let his performance on the court do the talking.

"You're a great basketball player," Crawford said, "and if you're as good as I think you are, you're going to shut them all up."

Whether or not Crawford remembered giving that advice, Wallace was heeding it, playing with a steady, calm sense of determination. With 14:33 remaining, he tipped in his own missed shot, then did exactly the same thing a minute later to ignite a 20–4 Vanderbilt run that put the game away for good. With just over two minutes remaining, now playing completely without fear, Wallace stormed downcourt on a fast break and whipped the behind-the-back pass to Warren for an easy layup, a move that was completely out of character.

This was all apparently too much to take for the Rebels, and on Vanderbilt's next possession, Wallace was hacked in the back of the head. Woozy from the blow, all he could do was stagger to the free throw line. He sank both shots.

Finally, Skinner pulled him from the game, his line score reading six for twelve on field goals, two for two on free throws, three fouls, eleven rebounds, four turnovers, one assist, and fourteen points. Final score, Vanderbilt 90, Ole Miss 72.

James Meredith had written that the most remarkable achievement of his time in Oxford was that he had survived. As he took a seat on the bench, Perry Wallace could relate.

Chapter 24

A River of Tears

EMERGING FROM THE INFERNO THAT was Mississippi, Wallace's third day in hell came on Sunday, February 11, at the church he'd attended most of his life, Schrader Lane Church of Christ. After the service, someone in the crowd called his name: "Perry! I heard they about lynched you down there in Mississippi!" The parishioners around him exploded in laughter. Wallace was shocked and angered by what he considered the "ignorant" and "outrageous" insensitivity of the moment. Even within his own community, there were those who mocked him, not grasping the full weight of his unique situation.

The fourth and final day in hell came on Monday, February 12, at Memorial Gym in the minutes before the Commodores' first practice since the win in Oxford. A voice rang out: "We're going to get you, boy!" A white student, thinking it was funny, began shouting out some of the same threats Wallace had heard at Ole Miss.

"It was bizarre and insulting," Wallace said. "This guy had actually been at the game and was a supporter down there. How could he have witnessed the horror of that event and still think it was funny to retrieve those moments with his mockery?"

Wallace later recalled his "Four Days in Hell" as the most symbolic and impactful ninety-six hours of his Vanderbilt career. "I was forced to be tougher, more protective of myself, and smarter about people," Wallace recalled. "I was changed greatly."

Nearly a month later, Perry Wallace sat in front of his locker, victorious yet completely depleted, his uniform drenched in sweat. Vanderbilt had just beaten LSU in the final game of the season, a 116–86 shoot-out that gave the Commodores their twentieth win of the year. Wallace had continued to play his best ball after his emotional performance in Oxford. He notched his first twenty-point-scoring game in an 84–73 win over Mississippi State, and then regained his starting position in the win over LSU, scoring eighteen points and grabbing twenty rebounds.

Vanderbilt *Hustler* sportswriter Henry Hecht considered

the LSU game as wild an affair as he had ever witnessed, and the pace of the game accounted for some of Wallace's perspiration. But there was more to it than that. As he sat on the folding chair, surrounded by teammates but all alone, a long, torturous season now over, it was finally time to exhale, to expel the physical, mental, and emotional pain he had endured all winter.

The rivers of sweat, he said many years later, might as well have been tears.

As he sat alone with his thoughts, an unexpected visitor arrived, and Wallace stood to greet a man who rarely entered the locker room.

"Perry," said Chancellor Heard, "I'd like to shake hands with you. Congratulations on the game and congratulations on the year."

Wallace would remember the words decades later, but more than anything, he would remember the look in the chancellor's eyes. "He was standing there in his usual gracious, elegant way, but there was also a great sense of sincerity," Wallace recalled. "As he stood there, something in his eyes told me that he really understood. No one else approached me with that kind of serious, sober, and sincere look. Nobody else seemed to understand that this had been a tremendously difficult year, a poignant year, and that I was as drenched with the effects of the whole experience as I was drenched with sweat from playing that game."

One other person who recognized what Wallace had endured was Hecht, the young sportswriter. A few days after the season finale, he sat down with Wallace to discuss—as he headlined his Sportsbeat column—"Perry's Long Season." Hecht was "impressed with the maturity and depth of this talented athlete as he gave himself a rigorous self-examination."

Wallace made no specific references to his painful experiences on the road, saying only that it "took me most of the season to get used to [it]." Though his life was unfolding in a far different way than he had imagined, Wallace downplayed his original high hopes. "I didn't sign [at Vanderbilt] to show or prove anything. It just happened that the school I wanted to go to was in the SEC."

Wallace told Hecht that his teammates were "really a great bunch of guys" who accepted him as a person, and credited Coach Skinner for never losing confidence in his abilities. In fact, Wallace said, "I wouldn't want to play for anyone else."

The young reporter wondered how Wallace would rate the year as a whole. "I guess I would have to say that it tended toward disappointing," Wallace said. "But I think I have made the adjustment I had to, and unraveled everything, and placed it in the right perspective."

Hecht posed one final question, one that Wallace would continue to be asked countless times over the ensuing decades: "Are you glad you came to Vanderbilt?"

Wallace answered honestly. "I probably won't know that for many, many years."

Chapter 25

Death of a Dream

PERRY WALLACE WAS ALONE IN his dormitory when his friend Walter Murray showed up to break the devastating news. Martin Luther King Jr. had been shot around 6:00 p.m. on April 4, 1968, as he stood on the balcony outside room 306 of Memphis's Lorraine Motel. Word of his assassination—at the hands of an unknown white suspect— spread quickly.

At first, Wallace refused to believe that what his best friend was telling him was true. As he began to process the news, everything seemed to go into slow motion, Murray's words becoming muffled, the room closing in, the world closing in.

"It was obviously just shocking at first, and then it became a feeling of profound sadness," Wallace recalled. "We just sat there and asked each other questions like, 'What are we going to do? What's going to happen now? Is this going to be the end of the civil rights movement?'"

Wallace and Murray each felt a personal connection to King. They had seen him up close at Vanderbilt almost exactly a year earlier, and while other young blacks had become enamored with more militant figures, the two friends remained devoted followers, invested in King's dream of equality.

Reaction to King's death took many forms around Nashville.

National Guardsmen ring the Tennessee State Capitol in the wake of the assassination of Martin Luther King Jr.

At Ireland's restaurant, some white patrons cheered when news of the assassination appeared on television. At Carmichael Towers, a group of frat boys walked up to the dormitory's roof so they could survey the action on West End and see what was happening across the tracks in the black neighborhoods in North Nashville. A student named Sara Hume was so frightened by the presence of army tanks sent into Nashville to prevent rioting that her whole body went numb. Another student, Marshall Chapman, looked on and thought, *We're at war, and the world's going to end.*

When Wallace saw photographs and television coverage of the crime scene in Memphis, he was reminded of an eerie coincidence: when his Pearl Tigers had played a game in Memphis two years earlier, the team had stayed at the Lorraine Motel—on the same floor and on the same side of the building as King. "It might seem silly and I'm not a superstitious person," Wallace recalled, "but that coincidence only multiplied the blinding . . . impact of King's assassination."

Memorials to King began to take shape around the country, including in Nashville, where Vanderbilt's Rev. Asbury worked to organize a service on campus, culminating in a march down West End Avenue.

Wallace wanted to participate, but he was also aware of the escalating racial tensions nationwide and on campus. He feared that his risky pioneering experiment could be ruined by even the slightest of misunderstandings. So while others around him and peers nationwide acted out of rage or sorrow, fear, or revenge, Wallace chose another course, mindful of what he considered his responsibilities as a trailblazer, fully aware of what he represented to blacks and whites alike. Some may have called his actions overly cautious, but in Wallace's view, he was taking the wisest approach.

"I actually went down and talked to one of the folks in the Athletic Department, [Sports Information Director] Bill Stewart, and I told him I wanted to participate in the march," Wallace recalled. "I saw Bill as a responsible adult that I could consult, and I told him that this was a peaceful march, expressing our sadness. This was not an angry march, not a riot, not violence-related. He said it was OK with him."

Those who were there say they will always remember the tears streaming down Walter Murray's face as Vanderbilt students, black and white, gathered outside Rand Hall for the on-campus memorial. Soon the mourners were on the move, more than two hundred strong, a group large enough to occupy the length of two city blocks as they made their way downtown. As the procession made its way closer to the downtown business district, the reassuring calm of the march was interrupted when a car came screeching by.

Wallace turned to see a carload of white teenagers hooting and hollering, and then one voice called out from the sedan,

"Your king is dead!" Wallace continued walking, reminded of a similar episode that had occurred five years earlier, when President John F. Kennedy was assassinated. Wallace had been walking home from Pearl High when another carload of celebrating rednecks zoomed by, one shouting, "Your nigger-loving leader is dead!"

Still, Wallace walked along in silence, impressed by the spirit of the group, a collection of young people with a great sense of responsibility and respect for the moment and for their country. "We wanted to in effect represent what Martin Luther King had represented, which was a calm, thoughtful, committed presence, with America's best interests in mind, and with the notion of human dignity and equality in mind," he recalled. "It was a wonderful coming together that we had, and we had a certain sense of calm as we marched. It was reassuring to us in a way, because we were really sad and distressed, and truly worried about what was going to happen now to our country."

Chapter 26

Truth to Power

WHETHER IT WAS OUT OF respect for King or in fear of continued riots, many segments of American life, including Major League Baseball games and the NBA playoffs, shut down in the days before and after his memorial service. Though it was highly unusual for so many games to be canceled following the death of a private citizen, the worlds of sports, politics, and civil rights were converging in many ways in the spring of 1968, even on the Vanderbilt campus. The case of Godfrey Dillard was a prime example. Dillard maintains that there have always been two sides to his personality. Ever since his mom brought home every conceivable type of sporting equipment when he was a kid, there has been the athletic side. But there has also been a political side, the aspect to his character that compelled him to travel south to college to play his part in the civil rights movement.

When his injured knee left him on the sidelines for the winter and spring of 1968, his political side grew dominant. He became heavily involved in the activities of the Afro American student association. His peers respected his brains and his ambition, electing him president of the association, and it was because he held this title that he was invited to address Vanderbilt faculty members in a specially called meeting on May 2. Dillard had grown increasingly frustrated with the slow progress of race relations on campus—this was his opportunity to speak truth to power, and he had no fear.

In his remarks and in subsequent interviews with the *Hustler*, Dillard discussed plans to hold "African culture days" and said he wanted to work with the administration to ensure that black contributions to American society were dealt with more honestly in history courses and that more black writers were studied in English classes. Explaining that part of his goal was to help white students understand that they were "part of the racial problem," he gave his thoughts on why the civil rights movement had evolved from nonviolence to Black Power.

"Demonstrations have outlived themselves as a force to build good attitudes in whites," he said. "I can't condemn anyone in the Black Power movement because the conditions of white society today made them what they are. The blame for Black

Power falls on the white man, because he has suppressed the black race to the extent that it will resort to violence. . . . If white society makes stable and programmed advances that people can see, then Black Power will die out. . . . Blacks are not content to stand still anymore."

Dillard's comments were persuasive enough that the faculty adopted his resolution to form their own race relations council. Still, his comments raised eyebrows. While he merely attempted to relay *warnings* about what might happen if progress weren't made, many at Vanderbilt interpreted his words as *threats*.

When Coach Skinner heard that Dillard was making controversial statements, he called Dillard into his office for a warning of his own. Skinner told Dillard that he needed to back off his political activities and focus just on basketball.

Dillard replied with an obligatory "OK," but in truth, the coach's words fell on deaf ears. "By that time, in my mind I sensed that they had soured on me," Dillard recalled. "They benched me, and then after I got hurt, I didn't feel like he wanted me back on the team, so I didn't feel very good about Skinner." Within a matter of days, there were whispers on campus that Dillard's days on the Commodore basketball team were numbered.

At the same time that Godfrey Dillard was attempting to advance the cause of black students on the Vanderbilt campus, a national political movement among black athletes, one Dr.

King himself had expressed support for, started gaining momentum. As Wallace continued his pioneering experiment in Nashville, the "plight of the black athlete" had became one of the most discussed topics in other parts of the country.

At the heart of this discussion, and at the center of the movement in which King had shown an interest, was a twenty-five-year-old sociology professor at San Jose State University named Harry Edwards.

Edwards was Black Power personified. He cut a provocative and imposing figure, standing an athletic six foot eight (he had first come to San Jose to play basketball and compete in track and field) and wearing a black beret and black sunglasses wherever he went. He came with street cred—growing up dirt poor in East St. Louis, Illinois, and spending time in jail, as his father and brother had.

Edwards, who had earned a master's degree at elite Cornell University, was a popular figure among students at San Jose State: his classes were jam-packed. At times, Edwards simply cited stark statistics to make his point that the sports world was no oasis of racial equality: there were no black managers in the Major Leagues or head coaches in the NFL; just one black head coach in the NBA; no blacks in the front office of any big league sport. Other times, he'd tell stories about how even the most famous black professional athletes were nonetheless denied homes and loans simply because of their race.

Edwards first organized a protest by black San Jose State football players in the fall of 1967, then expanded his efforts by creating the Olympic Project for Human Rights with the express purpose of organizing a black boycott of the upcoming Summer Olympics in Mexico City. Why should black athletes compete for the glory of the red, white, and blue on the world stage, Edwards asked, when they weren't treated as equal citizens at home?

Edwards never approached Perry Wallace, the only black athlete playing for a white college in the Deep South, but Wallace was well aware of Edwards's activities elsewhere. "I never had any personal exposure to him," Wallace said, "but as with most blacks, he was kind of a hero because here was a guy standing up, talking straight, and talking pretty tough. . . . I would have to say that I had a positive view of him, even though he was diametrically the opposite of me in the approach."

Just weeks after the basketball season ended, Wallace received a welcome visitor: a black reporter from *Sports Illustrated* who was helping compile research for a series *SI*'s Jack Olsen was writing on the status of black athletes, inspired in part by the work of Professor Harry Edwards. Wallace agreed to sit down for an interview, but under the condition he not be quoted by name in the story. Mindful of Dillard's recent experience, Wallace knew there could be bad consequences if word got out that he'd spoken critically of Vanderbilt.

"We talked about a number of different things—what it was like, what I was going through, what did I think of it, was I being let down, did I ever feel like leaving, and that kind of thing," Wallace recalled. "I told him that what I was experiencing was that either people were pretending that [racism] didn't exist, were denying it, or were getting angry if I said much about it."

When Olsen's series "The Black Athlete: A Shameful Story" ran in five consecutive issues in the month of July 1968, it instantly became the most controversial and talked-about piece in the magazine's history. Wallace read every word in the series, and though he was never mentioned by name, he recognized himself throughout, both because some of the material he provided was incorporated and because his experiences at Vanderbilt were so similar to the stories of other black athletes.

"Almost to a man, [black athletes] are dissatisfied, disgruntled and disillusioned," Olsen wrote. "Black collegiate athletes say they are dehumanized, exploited and discarded, and some even say they were happier back in the ghetto. Black professional athletes say they are underpaid, shunted into certain stereotyped positions and treated like sub-humans by Paleolithic coaches who regard them as watermelon-eating idiots."

In some ways, the articles drove Wallace into a deeper funk; on top of all the violence and hate in the world, here were five weeks of evidence that, in purely athletic terms, the situation was as bad or worse for other blacks as it was for him.

But in another sense, Wallace was energized by Olsen's series, just as he was by the movement organized by Harry Edwards, the mourning for Dr. King. In the midst of the madness that was 1968, at least people were talking about serious problems; at least they were confronting racial division as they never had before.

"There was a huge amount of turmoil at that time, but it came in the midst of some increased hope in terms of racial conditions," Wallace recalled. "There was a sense of finally being noticed as opposed to being ignored and invisible. . . . People were paying attention to blacks and issues that affected us. In and around the Vanderbilt campus, there were all these intelligent people, and many of them were really being stimulated into exploring these topics. They began to talk to us."

Chapter 27

The Cruel Deception

IN EARLY JULY OF 1968, Perry Wallace was asked to organize a meeting of the university's Human Relations Council (the group of white administrators and black students Heard had created) for the morning of July 25. As he read the *Sports Illustrated* articles over the course of the month, he realized he could use this opportunity to show that the incidents described in the stories weren't just easily dismissed, isolated problems at far-off schools.

The very fact that he planned to speak these words pointed to two other important truths: first, that despite his disappointment, he cared enough about Vanderbilt to try to improve the situation there; and second, that despite his fears regarding the potential consequences, he was confident enough to speak his mind in the most emotional speech of his life. He knew that if he held back in this setting, he would only be hurting the chances that things would change for the better.

Temperatures were climbing to ninety degrees on a humid Nashville morning when Wallace carried his notes into Chancellor Heard's office. The *Tennessean* newspaper had run a front-page story saying that in Cleveland, Ohio, black community leaders were patrolling the city in place of National Guardsmen, hoping to bring peace to an area where ten people were killed in rioting two days earlier. And here, standing before nine white men and women, stood a frustrated young black man who decided to use words, calmly spoken, to make a case not just for himself but for his classmates and those who would follow.

"The entrance of your first black athlete involved deception," Wallace said. "As I was sought after to attend Vanderbilt, many aspects of Vanderbilt life were not mentioned. Social life was one of them. I was simply brought in and expected to survive in an alien culture with no outlets for the originality of my own culture on campus.

"One of my other concerns was the degree of racism I would be shown in Deep Southern states. Certainly, I did not expect to have been given an experienced answer, but there was no need to avoid and cover up the issue by saying that it wasn't any worry at all. I was soon to find that this issue and the previous issue governing the social attitudes were to hamper my career and to affect my life viciously. . . . For you see, I trusted you and almost destroyed myself trying to prove that you were right."

As he continued, Wallace told stories about his mistreatment on campus. "My first year here involved a battle with my teammates to defeat their knowing and unknowing attempts to categorize me as the 'team nigger.' The fact that the coaches were not aware that certain things tended to stereotype me made it an even harder battle," he said. "I have already related to some of you the story of a teammate telling me of how I would surely have enjoyed the old slave breeding camps and asking me about picking cotton. What I didn't tell you was that a coach was present, and they all had a big laugh."

In describing his experience at Ole Miss, he showed that he knew his history was already being written; he wanted to set the record straight. "My game at the University of Mississippi is often lauded as one in which I bravely fought the racist catcalls and pestering to perform well and be cheered for at the end. But my thoughts of that experience hover around one series of events. I was hit in the eye during the first half; no foul was called and no officials' time-out was called when it could be easily seen that I was temporarily blinded in my left eye. In the locker room, I got treatment at halftime, but my teammates did not bother to wait . . . [for] me to return to the floor with them, and they forgot that I would have to return alone.

"Now, I don't expect you to attach much significance to merely having to run out on a basketball floor, but what I remember most in my life is standing at that huge doorway with that crowd waiting on me with my teammates completely at the opposite end of the floor. What would have merely been an occurrence of no consequence for a white player was transformed into a nightmare and a long, hellish trauma for me."

Wallace finished with the same sense of profound emotion with which he'd begun. "To sum it up, people, somebody has lied to me, somebody has deceived me, and it has resulted in the two unhappiest years of my life. . . . I don't say any of this to bring your sympathy and granted this has been a lengthy report, but surprisingly you have ignored much and the more blacks you have here, the more people you set up to face destruction.

"I ask, will you continue to try to destroy me and will you try to destroy others? Do you also think I'm going to sit and watch you destroy my black brothers and me? I'd rather turn into the monster you're making me than to go down without making some impact on what you've done. The articles in the magazine point out the problems, and it would be to Vanderbilt's advantage to take heed to them."

Wallace's words were at once painful, daring, and profound, but as he concluded his speech, his biggest worry was that his advice would be ignored. Indeed, it soon became clear that some in the room simply did not understand the depth of what he was saying.

One administrator attempted to convince Wallace that he was overreacting. "You know, Perry," the man said, "in these games, you might have the crowd giving a guy a hard time because he has red hair. They might call out, 'Red!'"

Wallace was angered by the comparison, and he shot back at the official. "There's a difference between calling a guy Red or whatever and calling me nigger. 'Red' is different than 'nigger.'"

The administrator was visibly upset by Wallace's retort, as was a senior Athletic Department official who called Wallace into his office days later. "You've got to admit that what we don't need is protest," the official said. "What we need is law and order."

"Yes, we do," Wallace replied, "any society needs law and order, but we also need justice. And the problem is that racism doesn't amount to justice. Bigotry doesn't amount to justice."

"If you feel so strongly about that, then why don't you leave?" the official said testily.

This could have been the end, the experiment to integrate the SEC over and done with. But Wallace understood the significance of his journey, even when this Vanderbilt leader did not.

"Sir, it's not my job to leave," Wallace replied. "It's not my job to get up and leave injustice in a country that claims to have justice. I have a right to be here like anybody else, and I'm not going to leave Vanderbilt."

Chapter 28

All Alone

EVER SINCE SUFFERING THE INJURY that sidelined him a year earlier, Godfrey Dillard had worked hard to rehabilitate his knee, preparing to regain a spot on the varsity in his junior year. By all accounts, he was succeeding. In a *Hustler* article on the team's summer workouts, Henry Hecht declared that "Godfrey Dillard looks to have made a complete recovery."

It could have been a simple story line: injured player works hard and is welcomed back with open arms. In reality, Dillard's return was quite complicated. As president of the Afro American student association, Dillard had become an outspoken student leader. While Wallace took a diplomatic approach in talking about issues of race on campus, Dillard never held back. When school started again in the fall, talk began to swirl among some pockets of alumni: Did Skinner really need to have this radical black kid from Detroit on the team?

Then there was Dillard's style of ball and his demeanor on the court—a flashier, brasher brand of guard play than Skinner was comfortable with. With the ball in his hands on virtually every possession, Dillard would be the face of the squad at a time when even integrated professional and Northern collegiate teams often restricted the number of black players on their rosters.

There was also the matter of numbers: sixteen players competing for no more than twelve spots on the roster. Whatever the reason, on the second day of practice before the 1968–69 season, Coach Skinner assigned Godfrey Dillard and four other teammates to the lesser B team, not the varsity. In speaking to the press afterward, Skinner said that the decision had been very difficult and that the B teamers would have the opportunity to work their way onto the varsity; nothing was final.

Dillard, however, felt that he hadn't been given a fair chance. The first day of practice had not even involved a scrimmage. On what basis was Skinner making his judgment?

"When they put me on the B team, it was obvious they did not want anyone to see me play," he recalled. "If they had allowed me to be out there on the floor, playing in front of the alumni, practice after practice, showing my talent in the scrimmages, they could not have kept me off the team." Dillard believed he was fighting a losing battle, but he decided he would play his hardest and see if he could earn a call up to the varsity.

As practices continued, Wallace was the team's most improved player ("Perry has shown at least a fifty percent improvement over last year," Skinner boasted), and Dillard took advantage of a rare opportunity to attract attention in a practice scrimmage, leading the B team back from a twenty-point deficit to beat the varsity substitutes.

But on November 24, with Thanksgiving and the season opener approaching, Skinner took stock of his roster, compared the performances of his varsity and B team players, and announced his final varsity lineup: Perry Wallace was named a varsity starter while Godfrey Dillard remained on the B team.

Nearly forty years after the fact, Skinner maintained that Dillard simply hadn't recovered fully from his injury.

Dillard disagreed. "It had been decided since the second day of practice that no matter what I did, no matter how I played, I was not going to be on the team."

If he wasn't going to be playing varsity basketball, Dillard believed there was no reason to stay at Vanderbilt, and he decided to transfer to a university back in Michigan.

First, though, he felt he needed to get Wallace's blessing. "That, to me, was the worst part of it—leaving Perry," Dillard recalled. "I knew he didn't want me to go, but he also knew what they were doing to me."

Wallace told Dillard that he understood, that he respected him for the decision he was making, that things would only get worse if he stayed.

After meeting with Wallace and other friends, Dillard called Detroit and talked to his mother and older brother, Kenneth, about what had happened. "Godfrey," his mother said, "you need to come on home."

Soon, Kenneth arrived in Nashville to pick up his little brother. At this point, Skinner still didn't know that Dillard planned to quit the team and withdraw from school, so Godfrey and Kenneth paid a visit to the coach's office.

"We went down there and I said to Skinner, 'You know you are doing me wrong, and I can't play for you again because you are discriminating against me. I don't know why you dislike me,'" Dillard recalled. "And he didn't say anything. He didn't say, 'Why don't you try to stick it out, maybe you can make it again.' He didn't give me any indication that there was any chance, which confirmed for me that nothing was going to happen."

Wallace felt the loss deeply. He had lost a close friend, once again left to tour the dangerous states of the South alone. But more significant, he was left to function within a team structure that he believed had just mistreated his fellow trailblazer.

"The whole thing with Godfrey was huge for me," Wallace

said. "We came in and planned to go through it together. The Mississippi State experience had been a bonding experience, in the face of all that hell. I come back the next year [my sophomore year] and I was by myself, but then I'm coming into my junior year thinking, 'Well, at least Godfrey and I are going to go through this thing together.' Then, not only is he not going to be on the team, but under these disturbing circumstances. These are the kinds of things that challenge your sense of faith. . . . I'm playing on a team that got Godfrey out because of race and politics? I just felt alone."

Wallace's anguish was compounded by the fact that his mother, Hattie, who had undergone surgery a year earlier, was still very sick. The cancer was making her weaker and weaker. For Perry, who had always been so close to his mom, her illness added another heavy load to the mental burden he carried as he contemplated another long year of basketball and an unforgiving engineering curriculum.

One more year to go. Could he make it?

Chapter 29

Nevermore

RAVEN! The air is clear of doubts.
Regroup and prepare for the long flight.
—Gustav

TUCKED AWAY ON THE BOTTOM of page 2 of the February 18, 1969, *Hustler*, the nonsensical, fifteen-word "Raven" ad, quoting some unknown "Gustav," was mysterious. Few people even knew that the student organization known as Raven even existed. Moreover, the lucky ones who were aware of Raven knew that there really *was no* Raven; in fact, it was just a fake secret club. Created during the mid-1950s, Raven was an elaborate prank that older students played on younger students.

Each year, the existing members of Raven identified thirteen unsuspecting upperclassmen to lure into their pretend club. The group was open to males only, and just a certain type of Vanderbilt man at that: the fraternity presidents, *Hustler* editors, student government leaders, Honor Council representatives, and top athletes who acted as if they owned the place, which made them the most likely people to fall for this type of prank.

As one former student put it: "They would explain to you that administrators and coaches and leading students were members of Raven, and that Raven was responsible for every big thing that had ever happened at Vanderbilt."

In the spring of 1969, near the end of Wallace's junior year, talk began to circulate among Raven members about which students should be recruited as a prank, or "fished," as they called it. Even though a black student had never been admitted before, one name that came up repeatedly, Raven leader Kevin Grady recalled, was Perry Wallace's best friend, Walter Murray.

"We were sitting around saying, 'Who is the next crop of suckers to bring in?' and Walter was an obvious choice," said Grady. "Walter was clearly within the zone to be fished [because he was a political leader on campus]. So we're sitting around and [fellow Raven member and classmate] Henry Hecht says, 'I think we ought to go for Perry Wallace, too.'"

And, with that, the process of recruiting Wallace and Murray began. On Murray's first day of class nearly three years earlier, he had been greeted as a "nigger." Wallace had suffered taunts in one gymnasium after another throughout the South. Both had spent countless hours with members of the administration pleading for better treatment of black students. Now they were told that they were being invited to join an elite organization that had the power to make bold changes on the Vanderbilt campus, led to believe that they could accomplish things through Raven that had been impossible to achieve before.

As with all the other Raven recruits, Wallace and Murray were invited to attend the group's upcoming initiation ceremony and ordered to wear white tuxedos for the occasion. When they arrived for the ceremony, Grady and his fellow members discussed the grand plans Raven had in the works, and then the new recruits were asked to stand and speak about what they hoped to accomplish through their participation with Raven.

"We go around the room," Grady recalled, "and when it comes to Walter Murray, he [says] he wants the university to become much more active in recruiting African American students. And then Perry stands up and says he'd never really felt comfortable at Vanderbilt, but that now he understood there was a lot he could do that he couldn't do before. . . . He opened his heart, and it quickly became clear that Perry was really serious about all this."

After all the students had spoken, it was time for the acts of initiation, carried out in an over-the-top fashion fitting for the occasion. As Raven member Chuck Offenburger recalled, at the end of what seemed like a very serious and important ceremony, "they tell you that Raven is [a made-up club]." There was no Raven organization accomplishing great things on campus; members never did anything else but attend this one party each year.

And this is when Raven's initiation ceremony veered off script. This was typically the point when the gullible young men who had been fooled into believing that they were about to join a powerful secret society realized that they had been tricked and began to smile. Maybe a few of the guys would be embarrassed or angry for just a few minutes, but with the punch line delivered and the tension let out of the room, the affair would quickly turn into a night of laughing and storytelling, everyone now in on the joke, bonding over their common experience, beginning to plot over whom to fish next.

Perry Wallace and Walter Murray reacted differently. They got up and left.

Chancellor Heard had reached the conclusion that in order for Vanderbilt's black students to have the same positive experience on campus as their white counterparts, special efforts would need to be taken. Many Raven organizers assumed that by treating Wallace and Murray just the same as the white classmates they were fishing, they were doing a good thing. Yet it was one thing to mislead a big man on campus who was part of the in-crowd, a white kid who felt comfortable at the university; it was quite another to lead on a pair of black students who were denied entry into the fraternities, who were greeted by slammed doors in their dormitories, who had experienced uncomfortable moments with the same students and administrators who now mocked them.

Where others could laugh at the elaborate hoax, Wallace and Murray were terribly disappointed, angry, and embarrassed to realize that they had poured their hearts out merely for the entertainment of the white men surrounding them. As they found out the hard way, Raven offered no promise of making life better for Vanderbilt's black students.

"It was very clear that Perry didn't like it at all," Grady recalled. "In retrospect, we had naïvely misunderstood the incredible pain that he had gone through, and how hard it was to be a black student and athlete at Vanderbilt. And then to stand up and unburden your soul, only to realize it's all a joke and to be laughed at—he didn't appreciate that one bit."

Looking back on the incident from a distance of more than forty years, Hecht is saddened by the role he played in setting up Wallace, a guy he'd considered his friend, for such a disappointment. "In our naïveté and immaturity, we didn't realize that it was a terrible thing to get his hopes up about changes at Vanderbilt," Hecht recalled. "It wasn't a joke to him. It was too important."

The Raven incident occurred in the final days of Wallace's junior year, meaning that he was nearly three-fourths of the way through his pioneering experiment at Vanderbilt. By this point, he had been stunned by the racism in Starkville, bloodied in Oxford. He had been booted from a church, asked to leave campus by a senior athletic official. Dr. King, a man he greatly admired, had been shot. His best friend on the team had been run off, and his mother was dying.

As the pressure created by all these events threatened to overwhelm him, Perry Wallace made a decision. Six months after Godfrey Dillard walked into Roy Skinner's office and announced his plan to leave Vanderbilt, Wallace approached the coach to say that he, too, wanted to leave the campus.

But there was a twist. In the first days of the summer of 1969, Wallace sat down with Skinner and posed a question: If he focused only on basketball, didn't bring up any racial issues or complain about anything during the season, would Skinner allow him to move into an off-campus apartment, to remove himself from the daily disappointments on campus that had made him so unhappy? Wallace knew that Skinner rarely granted such requests, but he promised he'd play the best basketball of his career if the coach agreed to his plan.

Skinner believed that Wallace was "mature enough" to thrive outside the structure the campus dorms provided and told Wallace that he had his blessing to find a new place to live. But he didn't stop there. He asked Wallace to stay in his office for a while, and together they devised a practice routine for the summer.

"He had me at five, seven, ten feet out, at the free throw line, so many hundreds of free throws every day, by myself in the gym, just for hours," Wallace recalled. "And that repetition was important. I say good things about Coach Skinner, and I mean all of it, but if I were to give an example of a real important contribution he made in my life, it would be the 'Roy Skinner ten-thousand-times rule,' and ten thousand times was how many times it seems that I shot that basketball every day."

Wallace believed the workouts offered a therapeutic way to deal with his mother's worsening health, a way of fighting back against whatever forces were taking her away. Working out by himself in the hot gym, Wallace found himself recapturing some of the "sweet peace" of the little boy who learned the game on the North High playground.

In the early days of August, right before the start of Wallace's senior year, this short-lived feeling of serenity was disrupted when tragedy struck. Surrounded by family members rotating in shifts, Wallace's mother, Hattie, passed away at Vanderbilt Hospital.

Wallace said that while his mother's death was a devastating event in his life, it also helped put the last year of his college experience in perspective. He was aware that he had just one last chance to accomplish many things: to prove himself as a basketball player, to graduate with his engineering degree, to finish his pioneering journey with pride.

Could he do all that?

Chapter 30

Bachelor of Ugliness

As colleges across the country opened their preseason basketball practices in October 1969, sportswriters identified the nation's top players. Despite the hours of work he had put in over the summer improving his game, Wallace, who had been one of the most highly touted sophomores when he joined the varsity, was no longer on the watch lists in his senior year.

Yet Wallace's teammates respected him deeply and elected him team captain. Skinner assembled his squad and declared his satisfaction with the vote by saying that Wallace "possesse[d] all the qualities of leadership required of being a captain of a Southeastern Conference basketball team."

As his teammates cheered, Wallace told a visitor that he

was "quite pleased" with the honor. "It is particularly reward-
ing to have been elected by this group, many of whom I
helped recruit when they came to visit the Vanderbilt campus," he said.

Wallace continued to take an active role in recruiting, particularly in the case of the few black basketball and football
players who visited Vanderbilt. Which isn't to say that Wallace covered up the truth of his experience. When a black basketball recruit named Tony Jenkins came down from Detroit,
Wallace explained what had happened with Dillard.

"I talked a lot about the Northern-Southern thing," Wallace recalled, "and how a lot of times the culture was still tied
enough to the old Southern world that if you didn't understand what I call 'The Song of the South,' then you could be in
some danger. Tony was someone who was bright and talented,
but he had some real reservations about coming down to a
Southern school. I told him that you've got some challenges on
campus, but it's workable." In the end, Jenkins chose to enroll
at Harvard.

Despite a mediocre finish (15-11) the previous season, fans
and experts were optimistic that the team would rebound in
1970; *Southern Basketball* magazine picked the Commodores to
win the SEC.

As the season rolled along, it was apparent that Wallace

Perry Wallace remains the lone black player in this senior-year team photo. Across the entire SEC, Auburn's Henry Harris was the only other black varsity basketball player that season.

VANDERBILT UNIVERSITY SPECIAL COLLECTIONS AND UNIVERSITY ARCHIVES.

had broken out of his shell as a player. He was blocking shots and rebounding as well as ever, but now his shooting had improved so much that he had become the team's most consistent scorer. He played with far less trepidation away from Memorial Gym: Henry Harris had joined the Auburn varsity as the league's second African American player, a handful of SEC schools now had blacks on their freshman squads, and the crowds became less rabid in their taunting. Memories of harsher experiences the previous three years served as motivation. Wallace would fondly remember walking off the court after playing in his final game in the state of Mississippi, looking up into the crowd, smiling, and thinking, *You didn't get me. And now I'm gone.*

But even as Wallace excelled on the court, it become obvious that, despite the high expectations for the Commodores, the team wasn't very good. Nobody seemed to be able to put their finger on why, but something just wasn't right: the team would win just twelve games and lose fourteen despite outscoring and outrebounding their opponents over the course of the entire season (proof that the only statistics that really matter are wins and losses!), the first losing season for Vanderbilt since 1948.

Along with the losing, Perry Wallace was forced to accept that his college career was coming to a close, and he began to think more seriously about his legacy, a task that became more difficult, not easier, as a slew of honors began coming his way. Not surprisingly, given his productivity on the court, Wallace would be named to the All-SEC second team upon the completion of the season. He would also receive the league's Sportsmanship Award, and the Vanderbilt faculty would present Wallace with an award of appreciation, recognizing his achievements in the classroom.

But it was another honor, this one voted on by Vanderbilt's

students, the award with the funny name, that created the greatest amount of angst for Wallace.

When he edged out his good friend Walter Murray to earn the "Bachelor of Ugliness" Award, Wallace understood more clearly than ever that the final chapter of his Vanderbilt story—as written by others—might be whitewashed with a happy ending that would forever hide the true nature of his experience. Though the name of the award sounds negative, the honor was actually bestowed to the male student who had "made the most significant contributions to the university."

But to Wallace, something about the whole experience felt *wrong*. He'd been declared the winner of a popularity contest, yet so few people on campus had even taken the time to get to know him.

"I remember when Perry started getting a lot of campus-wide honors," his teammate Bill LaFevor recalled. "It was a nice gesture, but there was a feeling that it was to make him feel better than he really needed to feel."

The award left Wallace feeling uneasy. "I began to feel that I needed to give people some idea about how things really had been because there was so much that people didn't know. People were about to wrap this thing up, this whole experience, into a nice, neat little package, just a quick civil rights success, like a pretty picture, and then put it away so they can forget about it and let it be like a trophy, as opposed to a work in progress where there is a tremendous amount of work that still remains."

Wallace believed he had a moral obligation to set the record straight. How would he do it?

Perry had a plan.

Chapter 31

He Saved the Best for Last

ON MARCH 7, 1970, THE day of Perry Wallace's final game, even the sun paid its respects, hiding behind the moon so that Wallace alone could shine. A solar eclipse dimmed all of Nashville from 11:35 a.m. until 2:35 p.m.; residents were warned not to look directly at the shrouded sun, lest they be blinded for life.

Coach Skinner said fans should gaze upon a different star—Wallace—and appreciate what they were witnessing for the final time. "It has been a most frustrating season," Skinner said. "I can't say I'm sorry to see the season end, but I'm certainly not happy that this is the last game we'll have Perry with us. He's been an outstanding young man both on and off the floor for four years."

As hard-core Vandy fan Harold Huggins settled into his seat just before tip-off, he wondered whether Wallace had read the letter he had mailed to him. *Dear Perry,* his letter began, *I've enjoyed your three years of varsity play at Vanderbilt, and I wish the best for you. What I would like for you to do in this last home game, and I know the rules say you can't dunk the ball, but I wish in the second half if Vanderbilt is ahead that you'd slam one in, and if the refs turn blue in the face calling technical fouls, then so be it.*

Huggins sat back and watched Vanderbilt's opponent take the court—it was none other than Mississippi State, the team that would forever occupy a haunted place in the minds of both Wallace and Godfrey Dillard, memories permanently etched of clutching each other's hands in a cramped, dirty locker room as courtside hecklers howled.

Wallace thought back to that first game in Starkville, about the scars he had accumulated over the last four years, the opportunities he had been denied; and most of all he felt the pain of his mother's death. He decided to dedicate this game to her, to play with extraordinary purpose and focus, to show the fans, and himself, what might have been possible had he been able to play free and easy all along. For one game, at least, it would be as if Perry Wallace were back on the court with the Pearl High Tigers, bringing a bit of the woomp show to Memorial Gymnasium.

The ball was tipped, and at first, it seemed that Wallace's

dream of a dazzling performance had been transformed into a nightmare. Everything was out of sorts—he was taking quick shots (and missing them), making mistakes that were completely out of character. Skinner recognized that Wallace was trying too hard, and he removed him from the game to regain his composure.

"And then," Wallace recalled, "I went to work."

When he checked back into the game, he played like a man possessed, scooping up every missed shot. By game's end, he had collected twenty-seven rebounds, just one short of Clyde Lee's school record. But Wallace didn't just rebound; his twenty-nine points were the most he had ever scored in a varsity game.

When the game was over, a 78–72 Commodore squeaker, the crowd serenaded Wallace with a standing ovation. As he stood and cheered, Harold Huggins had just one thing on his mind: Had Perry actually read his letter?

It sure seemed like it.

With Vanderbilt leading 74–70 with twenty-one seconds left in the game, Wallace found his opportunity to dunk when a teammate's shot skipped off the rim. Wallace leaped high for the rebound, caught the ball with one hand, and stuffed it in the basket.

"He did it because of me!" Huggins screamed.

Despite the illegal move, the referees swallowed their

whistles as the crowd roared with delight, allowing the bucket to stand.

The dunk was a crowd-pleaser, and it carried deep meaning to Wallace. Learning to play ball on the streets of North Nashville, leading an entire team of showstoppers at Pearl, the dunk had been Wallace's "freedom song," a provocative, forceful, and in its own way violent statement against inequality. And now here was Wallace's departing exclamation point.

As the crowd continued to bathe Wallace and his teammates in postgame cheers, teammate Steve Turner draped an arm over Wallace's shoulder, as if to protect his mentor.

Wallace maneuvered his way through a crush of children and fans who had stormed the court, stopping to sign autographs along the way, including one for Huggins, the letter writer. In the minds of those who watched him escape the court and duck through a doorway that led to the Commodore locker room, Wallace had completed his final act in grand style.

But he had an uneasy feeling in the pit of his stomach. "It was a sense of relief, but it was not an overwhelming joy," Wallace recalled. "It was more somber, because too much had gone on. It had been too difficult and too unresolved. I knew too much, and it weighed heavily on me."

While Wallace understood that it would be a long-term

challenge to deal with the painful feelings he had kept bottled inside for so long, he also recognized that in the short term he had unfinished business to take care of, business that might upset the fans who were now cheering for him.

That business, however, could wait a day. Wallace retreated to the embrace of family and friends in the locker room, where a reporter asked him what the high and low points had been in his career. He recounted the ordeal at Ole Miss as the most painful experience but recalled a recent encounter with a young black boy on the Vanderbilt campus as his most pleasant memory.

Walking to class, Wallace had been approached by the boy, who told him he was from Mississippi and had seen Wallace play on television. Ever since then, the boy told him, he had dreamed of going to college and playing basketball on TV just like Wallace. "That youngster and his determination to go to college is something that time will never erase from my memories of the last four years," he said. "It means something to inspire someone to climb up and do better things. Suddenly, all the hardships of being the first black athlete in the SEC [are] worthwhile."

Finally, after the kids had collected their autographs and the reporters had conducted their interviews, Wallace showered and dressed. As he walked out into a chilly Nashville night, his

Vanderbilt basketball career now over, he had never been more popular in this city.

Yet he knew that in less than twenty-four hours, he would sit down for an interview with a young *Tennessean* reporter and would "write his ticket out of town."

Chapter 32

Ticket Out of Town

Frank Sutherland was prepared to cook dinner. However long Perry Wallace wanted to talk, he'd listen, even if it meant taking a quick break to whip something up in his kitchen. Sutherland, a student at Vanderbilt and reporter for the *Tennessean*, had invited Wallace to his apartment for an afternoon interview.

During the final weeks of the basketball season, Wallace had decided that he wanted to publicly discuss the true nature of his pioneering experience. He had been the subject of newspaper coverage since high school, and he understood that if he wanted the everlasting record to reflect his feelings at this moment in history, the best way to accomplish that was by telling his own version of the story. He also understood that what he planned to talk about would anger a lot of people—so much so, he believed, that he would almost certainly not have the option of living and working in Nashville after graduation.

Wallace began to talk, and Sutherland scribbled in his notebook—no prepared questions, just a conversation. Wallace was as thoughtful, determined, and focused as he'd ever been on the basketball court.

"I didn't want to attack people, and I didn't want to bash the university," Wallace said decades later, "but I did want to speak in a way that objective people would see that this guy tried to tell the truth because it needed to be told, and he did it for the right reasons."

Stroking Sutherland's cat's soft black fur, Wallace began to speak. "It is ironic to be elected Bachelor of Ugliness because I have been a very lonely person at Vanderbilt. I can't say it any other way. I have been there by myself. Things have gotten a lot better over the years, but it has been a lonesome thing. . . . Over the years, many people knew my name, but they were not interested in knowing me."

Wallace picked up on the themes he had focused on in his emotional address to Chancellor Heard and the Human Relations Council two years earlier, telling Sutherland that his recruiters had "tricked" him into believing that the racial situation at Vanderbilt would present no problems.

Wallace talked about the toll Dillard's absence took on his

psyche—"He was one of the people I could look to for some understanding and friendship"—and of the difficulties of dealing with "racist" teachers. For the first time, he publicly shared the story of his banishment from the University Church of Christ.

Sutherland was taken aback by much of what Wallace said. "To be honest, I was really surprised about all of this at first, because I had just assumed, as had many other folks, that everything was all right. So when I heard this, I said, 'Oh, really?' Once I thought about it, I could understand it, but I had not thought about it [before], like a lot of other people."

Yet Wallace told Sutherland that his experience had not been all bad, claiming that "the fans have really been great" and that he had become closer to his senior-year teammates than he had with any other group.

Not once did he name names, nor did he mention the Raven experience, nor the athletic administrator's suggestion that he quit Vanderbilt if he was so unhappy. He could have said so much more, yet he anticipated the backlash that was sure to come.

"I know some people will say I am ungrateful," he told Sutherland, "but that's the way it has been. If I don't say this at some time in my life, it would be too much unbearable pressure."

And in his most emotional remarks, Wallace attempted to convey that the very fact that he was sitting there, speaking his mind, preparing to graduate, not diminished by bitterness, having completed a four-year tour of duty through a hostile South, all during a time of riots, war, and assassinations, had been no guarantee. "I have to say there were a lot of times in the four years I was trying hard when I got some bad breaks and a lot of disappointments—things went the wrong way. There is even now a thin line between success and failure. I would hate to have to do it again depending on just luck."

The interview went on for hours, Sutherland gaining confidence by the minute that he was onto something big. He was struck by Wallace's composure, feeling that the man he was talking to was "articulate, sensitive, aware, and hurt," more disappointed than angry. Closing his notepad, Sutherland thanked Wallace for his time and sped down to the *Tennessean's* office to begin writing his story.

Wallace returned to his apartment satisfied that he had accomplished his goals on two fronts. One, he had brought the university's racial difficulties out into the open. Lifting the lid, exposing the school's challenges to daylight, could only help improve things in the long run, he believed. Two, he had experienced a bit of the sense of closure he had hoped for, with "bit" being the operative word, considering all he had not said.

"It was amazingly contained as I look back at it," he recalled decades later. "But it was still bringing the message out and being less of the good, quiet, obedient Negro."

—————

Wallace woke up early on the morning of Monday, March 9, 1970, to buy a copy of the newspaper. There on the front page was a photo of him with Sutherland's kitten on his shoulder.

Walter Murray showed up at Wallace's door with a copy of his own, joking that all around town, people were probably picking up their *Tennessean* and running away in shock over what Wallace had said.

He was just about right.

All day long, Sutherland heard mixed reactions to what he knew was a bombshell of a story. Some people were angry at what they considered Wallace's lack of appreciation for the opportunities Vanderbilt had afforded him. Sutherland was accused by some of manipulating Wallace's words. One reader called Sutherland a "troublemaker," another wished Wallace "good riddance." Yet many of Sutherland's black friends called with words of support, telling him that nobody should be surprised by anything Wallace had said. Others were more curious than upset, surprised that Wallace had experienced such loneliness on campus: every time they had seen him, after all, he'd been surrounded by thousands of people in Memorial Gym.

More than anything, Sutherland began to realize, reader reaction was some combination of disappointment, sadness, anger, and exasperation. "I had been proud of Vanderbilt for being the first to bring in a black athlete, as had a lot of other people, but what this did in a lot of people's minds was negate some of the pride in that step because he wasn't happy," Sutherland recalled. "If this had been a male version of the Cinderella story, where he went off and was happy the rest of his life, they'd be able to say, 'Look what we did,' but the truth was that he had endured a lot more than people ever knew, so they couldn't be as proud of it, and that's what hurt a lot of the people who called me. They thought, as many folks did in the sixties and seventies, that once you've integrated with one person, you've done your job. . . . But that didn't mean the problems were solved."

And then there was the reaction of Roy Skinner, the country boy who'd been unable to deal with Godfrey Dillard. It was this man who read the story and came away with an opinion that wouldn't take hold as the lasting lesson from the whole episode for years to come. It was Coach Skinner who believed that Perry Wallace had been trying to help Vanderbilt, that he had done the school a favor by sharing his thoughts, that the basketball program and the university would be better for it in the long run.

"At first, I thought, 'How can he say all this stuff when they just voted you the most popular student?'" Skinner recalled. "But then the more I thought about it, I got real mad over how he talked about how he had been treated on campus. God, I don't know how he took it for four years. It was a lot worse than I thought it was. I felt for him, and I really admired him for doing it. He was trying to help us understand."

While Wallace's interview was his parting shot from a media perspective, he still had two months of school before he graduated. He turned his attention to finishing his coursework, ensuring that he would receive his engineering degree. He also wanted to give professional basketball a shot, should he get the opportunity. Though he understood the limitations to his game, with dunking allowed and black players commonplace, pro ball would be a completely different ball game.

In late March, Wallace was selected in professional drafts by both the Philadelphia 76ers of the NBA and the Kentucky Colonels of the rival American Basketball Association. Four years earlier, he'd agonized over whether to remain in the South for college or whether to fulfill his dreams of finding opportunity in an integrated Northern setting, and he had decided to stay home. This time, he didn't have to think twice about whether to go to Kentucky or Pennsylvania: he'd join the 76ers right after graduation.

The skies were heavy with thunder on May 31, 1970, Vanderbilt's graduation day, forcing the commencement ceremonies inside. Wallace knew how much this moment meant to his father, how much it would have meant to his mother. He put on his cap and gown and, along with 1,412 fellow graduates, made one final appearance in Memorial Gym.

Wallace had survived an experiment that might have ended tragically if not for his uncommon self-awareness, intelligence, sensitivity, strength, and grace. There was much to celebrate as he graduated from an esteemed university.

But as Wallace and his best friend, Walter Murray, hurriedly left the gym and changed out of their caps and gowns, Murray taking the wheel of his green Dodge, Wallace riding shotgun for a trip to the airport and a flight to Philadelphia and rookie camp with the 76ers, any joy he felt was bittersweet, tempered by the death of his mother, the experiences of the last four years, and the knowledge that once his plane lifted off, time and distance would forever change the nature of his relationship with his best friend, no matter how much they swore it wouldn't.

As they drove on toward the airport, Murray leaned over and turned on the car radio. On came a song by the popular musical trio Peter, Paul and Mary. The two old friends turned toward each other, smiled, and shared one last laugh as they listened to the chorus.

I'm leaving on a jet plane, I don't know when I'll be back again.

AUTHOR'S NOTE

What became of Perry Wallace after his Vanderbilt days were over?

As one might suspect, his life has been one of continued challenges and accomplishments, all leading to what he considers his greatest achievement.

When he flew north to Philadelphia after his graduation ceremony, Wallace wanted nothing more than to prove his basketball doubters wrong, to see if he could thrive in the NBA, where dunking was allowed and he could play without the anxiety he'd experienced at Vanderbilt. He would indeed perform well at rookie camp but was not too surprised when 76ers coach Jack Ramsay told him he would not make the team, which was loaded with talented veterans. Still, Ramsay admired Wallace's intellect and determination, and he told him that he would write a letter of recommendation if Perry decided to attend law school, as Perry had discussed doing.

And, indeed, that's the path Wallace chose, earning his law degree from prestigious Columbia University in New York. After serving the country as a member of the National Guard and as an attorney for the United States Department of Justice, Wallace became a professor, first at George Washington University, then at the University of Baltimore, and finally at American University in Washington, D.C., where he is now a highly regarded professor at the university's law school. The education Perry Wallace received from his family and from his

Wallace is now a professor of law at American University in Washington, D.C.
PHOTO BY LISA NIPP, THE TENNESSEAN.

dedicated teachers at Pearl High School, Vanderbilt, and Columbia has served him well.

Perry Wallace says the most important decision he's ever made in his life, far more important than his decision to attend Vanderbilt and desegregate SEC basketball or to take any of the jobs he has been offered, was when he and his wife, Karen, chose to adopt a daughter in early 1992. They named the baby Gabrielle Eugenie Wallace, a tribute to Karen's mother's maiden name, Gabriel, and a French spin on the middle name Perry had inherited from his father: Eugene.

As Gabrielle grew up, it became obvious that she was different from other kids her age. She wasn't talking and wouldn't answer when her parents called her name. Eventually, doctors determined that Gabby had Asperger's syndrome, a high-functioning form of autism marked by extreme social challenges.

And here, at this low point, is where the course of Perry Wallace's life turned back upon itself. All that he had experienced as a child growing up in a segregated society, all the suffering as a pioneer, all the healing in the years since—he now saw all of this in a new context, making him the ideal adoptive father for this little girl. Wallace's own parents had lived with a determination that their children would not be limited by the circumstances of their birth, and now it was his turn to take the same approach with his daughter.

Gabby would not make eye contact. It reminded Wallace of his childhood in Nashville, where looking a white man in the eye was inviting trouble. Gabby was taunted by some of her schoolmates for being different, reminding Wallace of the threats he had received his whole life, from the black kids who'd thought he was a Goody Two-shoes to the nasty crowds in places like Athens, Knoxville, and Baton Rouge. Gabby had the hardest time learning to tie her shoelaces. Patiently working with his daughter reminded Wallace of the methodical approach to schoolwork that had been so common in the schools of North Nashville during his childhood, where teachers were determined to help their students overcome generations of discrimination.

As there had been at Vanderbilt, there were good days and bad, moments of joy and crushing disappointment, lots of hard work with no guarantees that it would pay off. At their lowest points, Perry and his wife, Karen, held hands, like Wallace and Dillard had in Starkville, and vowed that together they'd find the strength to make it through.

As Wallace moved along with his career and family, he also began to receive some long overdue recognition for the history he made at Vanderbilt. After graduating in 1970 and speaking out in the *Tennessean*, he wasn't invited back to campus to be honored or to talk about his experience until 1989.

But finally, as people and attitudes changed, Wallace was welcomed back as a member of the Vanderbilt family. Then, in 1995, Wallace was named to the National Association of Basketball Coaches' Silver Anniversary team, and in 1996, he was presented a "sports pioneer" award by Reebok and the National Association of Black Journalists.

A few years later, a group of Vanderbilt students became determined to do something to honor Wallace. They talked to Vanderbilt athletic director David Williams about what could be done, and an idea was proposed. What about retiring Wallace's jersey so that no other Vanderbilt player could ever wear it again and hanging an oversized version from the rafters at Memorial Gym as a way to honor him?

"Perry Wallace is a hero," Williams said. "There's no other way to say it. He's a hero. Perry did more for Vanderbilt than Vanderbilt ever could have done for him."

In addition to retiring Wallace's jersey, Vanderbilt would in future years name a dormitory after his friend Walter Murray, induct Wallace into the inaugural class of the Vanderbilt Athletic Hall of Fame, establish an engineering scholarship in his honor, and create the Perry Wallace Courage Award to recognize student-athletes overcoming significant challenges.

But first came the jersey retirement, set to take place just before tip-off of a February 21, 2004, game against LSU. The mayor of Nashville proclaimed it "Perry Wallace Day." Karen

Perry Wallace is flanked by Godfrey Dillard and Bill Ligon at Wallace's jersey retirement ceremony on February 21, 2004.

VANDERBILT UNIVERSITY ATHLETIC DEPARTMENT.

and Gabby made the trip from Washington, D.C., and there, too, was Godfrey Dillard, now a successful attorney and judge, back on campus for the first time in decades.

While the ceremony brought Perry Wallace some sense of closure, it would only just begin that process for Dillard; but begin it did. Earlier in the day of the jersey retirement, Dillard attended a campus luncheon. After the emcee introduced Dillard to the crowd, an aging professor approached him.

"Godfrey, I want to apologize for what happened to you," the man said. "Not everybody agrees with what happened to you at that time."

In the years that followed, Dillard would be written back into Vanderbilt's history, occasionally coming back to campus to meet with student groups. Speaking to a black fraternity, he told the students that although he believed he had been shortchanged in terms of his athletic career, he did not allow that to stifle his dreams.

"I told them failure or setbacks do not have to be the end of the game," he said. "It can be an opportunity, a chance for a fresh start—a new beginning. What is necessary is a realistic assessment of who you are, what you want to be, and how to get there. I told them I decided that I was going to make those choices, not somebody else. So, I picked myself up, dusted myself off, and went to work at being happy."

Surrounded by thousands of Vanderbilt fans for the first time since 1970, Perry Wallace stood in the center of the familiar, wide court. The fans all stood in respect as the replica jersey was unveiled. Wallace was handed a microphone.

"Many years ago, Vanderbilt and I set out on a great and ambitious journey," he said. "A journey about progress and about justice. And tonight we celebrate that journey's great success."

The crowd of 13,892 erupted in applause, and Wallace turned and waved to each corner of the gymnasium, then gazed up at the suite where Karen and twelve-year-old Gabby waved back. At his core, Wallace was more than a pioneer, more than a symbol: he was a husband and father. Though no one in the gym besides Karen and his other family members knew it, it was in his love and devotion to Gabby that Perry Wallace had made his most satisfying—and most difficult—contribution to this world.

At this moment, he understood that his happy ending was ultimately not about public victories, not about being recognized by others for what he'd accomplished as a sports and civil rights pioneer, but rather was about private victories, within his own family. Despite the challenges of Gabby's childhood, the Wallaces worked hard to provide her the best possible opportunities and education, finding extra money each year to pay for special services and tuition at a school that specialized in serving highly intelligent kids with disabilities.

And gradually, she made progress.

In the years that followed the jersey retirement, under-standing of Asperger's began to improve, and along with the scientific milestones came moments of joy at home, Gabby discovering a love for art and computers. She began to enjoy school and became more comfortable around her teachers and classmates, eventually becoming an honor student, graduating from high school, and enrolling in a nearby college. For Wallace, a man who knows a thing or two about beating the odds, Gabby's progress has been his life's most important victory.

"It's the closest thing to a miracle we have ever experienced," Wallace said. "We have won, and won big."

ACKNOWLEDGMENTS

This adaptation of *Strong Inside* would not exist but for the encouragement and extraordinarily kind assistance of the amazing, best-selling author Ruta Sepetys. After a chance introduction to Ruta at a Nashville coffee shop, she took me under her wing for no other reason than to be helpful to a person with a story she believed needed to be heard by young readers.

Ruta then introduced me to her editor at Philomel, the legendary Michael Green. Thank you to Michael for believing that Perry Wallace's story could translate so well to the young reader format, and to the brilliant Brian Geffen, my editor who helped make this book shine. Also at Philomel, I appreciate the hard work of publicist Bridget Hartzler, copy editor Cindy Howle, and designers Tony Sahara and Kimi Weart. Thank you also to Alice Lawson at the Gersh Agency, a wise guide in the publishing world, and to everyone at Vanderbilt University Press, terrific stewards of the adult version of this book. Thank you to the booksellers, librarians, and teachers who continue to deliver *Strong Inside* to so many readers, and to everyone in Nashville who has embraced both versions of this book—and me—so warmly. This whole experience has left me with no doubt that I live in one of the country's greatest "book towns," not to mention a wonderful place to raise a family.

I am grateful for this opportunity to thank my teachers for helping me develop my writing skills over the years at Slackwood (Lawrenceville, New Jersey), Janney (Washington, D.C.), and Four Corners (Silver Spring, Maryland) elementary schools; Eastern Junior High (Silver Spring); and Austin (Texas) High School. And I am eternally grateful that my Vanderbilt University professor Dr. Yollette Jones encouraged me to write about Perry Wallace in the first place—as a sophomore at Vanderbilt in 1989.

Thank you to Perry Wallace, who means far more to me than just the subject of this book. Professor Wallace has been a teacher, mentor, business advisor, confidant, and father figure, and I count myself extremely lucky to have had him play such an important role in my life ever since I was a teenager.

Finally, it is one of the best perks of writing books to have the chance to thank one's family in such an immortal way

(I think plumbers should get to leave acknowledgments on pipes). Thank you to my parents, David and Linda, for unconditional love—and for a house where books and reading were valued—and to my sister, Sarah, the true artist in the family. In Doug and Cathy Williams, I have the world's greatest in-laws, and the best thing they ever did was create Alison, a beautiful person in every possible way and the heart, soul, and strength of our little family.

And finally, I get to tell my silly, smart, and sweet children, six-year-old Eliza and three-year-old Charlie, how much I love them. Nobody in our family reads more books than they do—can't wait for their review of this one in a few years. Oh, and one last thing. Thanks to Eliza's imaginary friend, Seepie, and Charlie's stuffed dog, Chewadi. Kiddos, may you never lose your wonderful imaginations, nor your love for the people and things (even imaginary or stuffed) that comfort you.

BIBLIOGRAPHY

INTERVIEWS

Jacqueline Akins, Steven Ammann, Tom Arnholt, Bev Asbury, Bob Baldridge, Hal Bartch, Vereen Bell, Bob Bundy, Leonard Burg, Bob Calton, Rick Cammarata, Eileen Carpenter, Marshall Chapman, Jim Combs, Eddie Crawford, Don Dahlinger, Jimmy Davy, Godfrey Dillard, Dan Due, Walter Fisher, Rod Freeman, Frye Gaillard, Bessie (Wallace) Garrett, Patrick Gilpin, Joel Gordon, Kevin Grady, Tom Hagan, Christie Hauck, Lee Hayden, Cornelia Heard, Henry Hecht, Sam Heys, Harold Huggins, Sara Hume, Jessie (Wallace) Jackson, Kathleen (Gallagher) Kemper, Steven Kendall, Don Knodel, Kassian Kovalcheck, Paul Kurtz, Bill LaFevor, Clyde Lee, Bill Ligon, David Lombard, Van Magers, Steve Martin, Paul Menzel, Tony Moorman, Carolyn (Bradshaw) Morgan, Morris Morgan, Donna Murray, Roy Neel, Chuck Offenburger, Bobbie Jean Perdue, Dick Philpot, K. C. Potter, John Seigenthaler, Roy Skinner, Billy Smith, Gene Smitherman, Jerry Southwood, Frank Sutherland, Annie (Wallace) Sweet, Willie Sweet, Keith Thomas, Terry Thomas, John Thorpe, Curry Todd, Pat Toomay, Bill Traughber, Michael Vinsang, Karen (Smyley) Wallace, Perry Wallace, Bob Warren, Paul Watermulder, Bedford Waters, David Williams, Rod Williamson, Paul Wilson, Bo Wyenandt, Linda Wynn.

BOOKS

Abdul-Jabbar, Kareem, and Peter Knobler. *Giant Steps: The Autobiography of Kareem Abdul-Jabbar.* New York: Bantam Books, 1983.

Bass, Amy. *Not the Triumph but the Struggle: The 1968 Olympics and the Making of the Black Athlete.* Minneapolis: University of Minnesota Press, 2002.

Boyd, Todd, and Kenneth Shropshire, eds. *Basketball Jones: America above the Rim.* New York: New York University Press, 2000.

Bradley, Michael. *Big Blue: 100 Years of Kentucky Wildcats Basketball.* Saint Louis: Sporting News, 2002.

Burt, Jesse C. *Nashville: Its Life and Times.* Nashville: Tennessee Book Company, 1959.

Carey, Bill. *Chancellors, Commodores, and Coeds: A History of Vanderbilt University.* Knoxville, TN: Clearbrook Press Publishing, 2003.

Carson, Clayborne. *In Struggle: SNCC and the Black Awakening of the 1960s.* 1981. Reprint, with new introduction and epilogue. Cambridge, MA: Harvard University Press, 1995.

Conkin, Paul K. *Gone with the Ivy: A Biography of Vanderbilt University.* Knoxville: University of Tennessee Press, 1985.

Doyle, Don H. *Nashville since the 1920s.* Knoxville: University of Tennessee Press, 1985.

Doyle, William. *An American Insurrection: The Battle of Oxford, Mississippi, 1962.* New York: Doubleday, 2001.

Edwards, Harry. *The Revolt of the Black Athlete.* New York: Free Press, 1969.

Eig, Jonathan. *Opening Day: The Story of Jackie Robinson's First Season.* New York: Simon and Schuster, 2007.

Fitzpatrick, Frank. *And the Walls Came Tumbling Down: Kentucky, Texas Western, and the Game That Changed American Sports.* New York: Simon and Schuster, 1999.

Gaillard, Frye. *With Music and Justice for All: Some Southerners and Their Passions.* Nashville: Vanderbilt University Press, 2008.

George, Nelson. *Elevating the Game: Black Men and Basketball.* Lincoln: University of Nebraska Press, 1992.

Graham, Tom, and Rachel Graham Cody. *Getting Open: The Unknown Story of Bill Garrett and the Integration of College Basketball.* New York: Atria Books, 2006.

Guthman, Edwin, O., and C. Richard Allen, eds. *RFK: Collected Speeches.* New York: Viking, 1993.

Halberstam, David. *The Breaks of the Game.* New York: Knopf, 1981.

———. *The Children.* New York: Random House, 1998.

Harris, Mark. *Pictures at a Revolution: Five Movies and the Birth of the New Hollywood.* New York: Penguin, 2008.

Haskins, Clem, with Marc Ryan. *Clem Haskins: Breaking Barriers.* Champaign, IL: Sports Publishing, 1997.

Haskins, Don, with Dan Wetzel. *Glory Road: My Story of the 1966 NCAA Basketball Championship and How One Team Triumphed Against the Odds and Changed America Forever.* New York: Hyperion, 2006.

Heard, Alexander. *Speaking of the University: Two Decades at Vanderbilt.* Nashville: Vanderbilt University Press, 1995.

Jacobs, Barry. *Across the Line: Profiles in Basketball Courage: Tales of the First Black Players in the ACC and SEC.* Guilford, CT: Lyons Press, 2008.

Katz, Milton S. *Breaking Through: John B. McClendon, Basketball Legend and Civil Rights Pioneer.* Fayetteville: University of Arkansas Press, 2007.

Maraniss, David. *Rome 1960: The Olympics That Changed the World.* New York: Simon and Schuster, 2008.

Meredith, James. *Three Years in Mississippi.* Bloomington: Indiana University Press, 1966.

Neel, Roy M. *Dynamite: 75 Years of Vanderbilt Basketball.* Nashville: Burr-Oak Publishers, 1975.

Northington, Nathaniel, with La Monte McNeese. *Still Running: The Autobiography of Kentucky's Nate Northington, the First African American Football Player in the Southeastern Conference.* Bloomington, IN: iUniverse, 2013.

Olsen, Jack. *The Black Athlete: A Shameful Story: The Myth of Integration in American Sport.* New York: Time-Life Books, 1968.

Pearce, Gene. *Field of Dreamers: Celebrating Tennessee High School Sports.* Hermitage, TN: Tennessee Secondary School Athletic Association, 2005.

Ramsay, Dr. Jack. *Dr. Jack's Leadership Lessons Learned from a Lifetime in Basketball.* Hoboken, NJ: John Wiley and Sons, 2004.

Rhoden, William C. *Forty Million Dollar Slaves: The Rise, Fall, and Redemption of the Black Athlete.* New York: Three Rivers Press, 2006.

Rice, Russell. *Adolph Rupp: Kentucky's Basketball Baron.* Champaign, IL: Sagamore Publishing, 1994.

Rosen, Charley. *Scandals of '51: How Gamblers Almost Killed College Basketball.* 1978. Reprint, New York: Seven Stories Press, 1999.

Russell, Fred. *Fifty Years of Vanderbilt Football.* Nashville: Fred Russell and Maxwell E. Benson Publishers, 1938.

Sansing, David G. *The University of Mississippi: A Sesquicentennial History*. Jackson: University Press of Mississippi, 1999.

Traughber, Bill. *Vanderbilt Basketball: Tales of Commodore Hardwood History*. Charleston, SC: History Press, 2012.

Ward, Geoffrey C. *Unforgivable Blackness: The Rise and Fall of Jack Johnson*. New York: Knopf, 2004.

Wendel, Tim. *Summer of '68: The Season That Changed Baseball—and America—Forever*. Cambridge, MA: Da Capo Press, 2012.

Wiggins, David K., ed. *Out of the Shadows: A Biographical History of African American Athletes*. Fayetteville: University of Arkansas Press, 2006.

NEWSPAPERS/MAGAZINES

Atlanta Constitution

Daily Mississippian

Jackson Clarion-Ledger

Lexington Herald-Leader

Los Angeles Times

Louisville Courier-Journal

Massachusetts Review

Nashville Banner

Nashville Business & Lifestyles

Nashville Scene

New York Times

Sports Illustrated

Tennessean

Tennessee Register

Urban Journal

Vanderbilt Alumnus

Vanderbilt Hustler

Vanderbilt Magazine

Vanderbilt Register

Washington Post

ARCHIVES

Nashville Public Library Special Collections

Tennessee Secondary School Athletic Association

University of Mississippi Athletic Department Archives

Vanderbilt University Athletic Department Archives

Vanderbilt University Special Collections & Archives

INDEX

M

Maloy, Mike, 151

Maravich, "Pistol" Pete, *167*

McClain, Ted ("Hound"), 31, 41, 60, 61

McClennon, Cynthia, 123

Memorial Gym (Vanderbilt University), 36, 49, 53, 58, 62, *63*, *65*, 147, 151, 163

Meredith, James, 3, 107, 172, 178

Middle Tennessee State University, 100–101

Mississippi State Bulldogs, 1, 3–4, 222

mononucleosis, Vanderbilt Commodores sick with, 154–155, 157–159

Moorman, Tony, 35–36, 44, 64

Morgan, Morris, 83, 135, 140

Municipal Auditorium (Nashville, TN), 36–37

Murray, Donna, 29

Murray, Walter, 87, 130, 139, 184–185, 187, 208–211, 231, 234, 239

N

North High School, 10, 17–18

Northwestern University, 46

O

Offenburger, Chuck, 210

Ole Miss (University of Mississippi) Rebels, 3, 99–100, 171–178, 198–199

Olsen, Jack, 193–194

Owens, R. C., 142–143

P

Parham, Ron, 39

Pearl High School

    1966 state tournament, 57–64, *63*, *65*

    band, 22–23

    first school game between a white team and a black team, 35–41

    quality of education, 25–29

    "separate but equalized" education, 27–29

    teachers' relationships with students, 27–29